COOKING DONEGAL RAPESEED

Compiled and Edited by Rhonda Laird, Donegal Rapeseed Oil

Designed by Aidan Spence

Printed by Browne Printers

Copyright © Donegal Rapeseed Oil 2017

www.donegalrapeseedoil.com

All rights reserved. No part of this book may be reproduced, used in any other publication, stored in a retrieval system or transmitted in any form or by any means without prior permission in writing from the publisher.

ISBN: 978-1-5272-1203-9

Aidan Spence
Freelance Designer
Telephone: 086 1025538
info@aidanspence.ie
www.aidanspence.ie

Browne Printers
Joe Bonnar Road, Letterkenny, Donegal
Telephone: 074 9121387
reception@browneprinters.com
www.browneprinters.com

FOREWORD

Donegal is well known for its hospitality and beautiful scenery but we are modest when it comes to boasting of our industry & business success. Donegal Rapeseed Company was established in 2009 and came about when Austin Duignan, Managing Director, realised that almost all of the cooking oil used in Ireland was imported and the unique soil in the area was ideal for growing the rapeseed crop. Stephen Allen, Director, teamed with Austin to lend his vast knowledge of food production and together they developed the idea to produce an Irish Cold Pressed Rapeseed Oil. There was work to be done in educating people of the many health benefits and of the wide range of uses from baking, dressings and roasting being a favourite with the higher smoke point. People were very quick to respond and Donegal Rapeseed Oil became a firm favourite in homes and restaurants throughout the country.

Donegal Rapeseed Oil is cold pressed which simply means that the oil is gently extracted by pressing the seed and without the use of solvents or chemicals. The oil is a pure product, produced with nothing added or taken away, this results in the golden colour and with the local growing conditions provides a light and delicate flavour enjoyed by all.

We are all becoming more concerned about the type of food we eat and how we cook and Donegal Rapeseed Oil is the healthy choice with no artificial colours, flavours or preservatives and is a natural source of essential omega fats. These omega fats help to maintain normal cholesterol levels in the body, which is important for cardiovascular health. It is also a rich source of vitamin E, which is a natural antioxidant. Donegal Rapeseed Oil contains 8 times more omega 3 and less than half the saturated fat of olive oil, making it one of the healthiest culinary oils on the market.

We have compiled this range of recipes with the help of many of our loyal customers and followers to show the variety of uses of Donegal Rapeseed Oil in response to the many comments and questions we receive when attending food shows and tastings. We hope you enjoy them as much as we do.

We are donating sale proceeds of this book to three great charities and we thank you for your support.

JEAN LAIRD

DONEGAL RAPESEED OIL

Cumann Alzheimer na h-Éireann

County Donegal Branch

Brainse Chondae Dhún na nGall

Coinnigh cumihne orthu sin na bhfuil cuimhne orthu

THE ALZHEIMER SOCIETY OF IRELAND

With three or four new cases of Alzheimer's or related dementias being diagnosed each week in County Donegal, the work of The Alzheimer Society of Ireland (Donegal Branch) is needed more than ever. In the 25 years since the foundation of the Donegal Branch, they have helped hundreds of families to cope with the condition. About 180 families are currently being helped out of the 2,200 families affected by the illness in the county, a number that will rise to 5,000 families by 2035.

About 57,000 hours of care was provided in 2016 primarily through home respite care but also through Day Care (at Gaoth Dobhair, Glenties and Cloghan), Social Clubs (at Letterkenny, Ballyshannon, Fanad and Moville) and a limited number of night time or weekend breaks. However the Branch has 92 families currently waiting for care.

In 2017, Alzheimer cafes, Cognitive Training and additional Family Carer Training sessions are being launched in order to try and provide some help to the maximum number of families possible. Cognitive Training will be especially useful for the 10% of people diagnosed with early onset dementia (under 65 years of age) as the Branch is aware of many cases from their 30's to early 60's with the illness. However, it is only through additional home care hours that the Branch will be able to provide the best help in a county as large as Donegal.

To contact the branch, email donegal.branch@alzheimer.ie.

For information about Alzheimer's and related dementias, call +35374 9722795 (Donegal Branch) or 1 800 341 341 (Confidential Helpline).

WWW.ALZHEIMER.IE

ALASTAIR MCKINNEY
CHAIRPERSON, THE ALZHEIMER
SOCIETY OF IRELAND

GOOD & NEW
In Aid of Donegal Cancer Patients & Their Families

THE GOOD AND NEW CANCER BUS

For cancer patients in the North West, treatment involves a very long road trip. Some will travel 600km in a week to get to the nearest cancer care centre and back. Eoin Butler from the Irish Times boards the charity cancer bus in Letterkenny and talks to patients bound for treatment in Galway.

Its 7.15am at the Dry Arch filling station in Letterkenny and a hard frost is down outside. Out on the forecourt, Eamon McDevitt is running through the names on today's passenger list. A cancer survivor himself, he has been providing a free bus service for Donegal patients requiring radiation treatment at University College Hospital, Galway for more than three and a half years.

It seems incredible, on such a tiny island, that cancer patients should have to travel such distances to receive treatment. McDevitt agrees. "Imagine a map of Ireland," he says. "Draw a line from Galway in the west to Dublin in the east. There are eight cancer centres of excellence below that line and zero above it."

At 7.30am, McDevitt's 22-seater coach pulls out onto the N13. The passengers are mostly older people. Some are travelling on the bus for the first time. They have loved ones to see off and baggage to stow. But delays are kept to a minimum. Everything proceeds with military precision.

Eoin asks McDevitt about the proposed radiotherapy facility at Altnagelvin Hospital in Derry. "We were promised Altnagelvin in 2009. Then it was put back to 2010. Then we were guaranteed it would happen in 2012. As far as we're concerned in Donegal, we're not holding any faith in it." In the meantime, his Good and New Cancer Group charity continues to muddle along as best it can. "It costs about €1,000 a week to keep this service going. Right now, we have enough money in the kitty to keep us going another four and a half weeks." The group fundraising is mostly done by former patients.

We've made it to Galway in just under four hours. The following evening, Eoin speaks to McDevitt on the phone. He mentions AXA Insurance in Letterkenny, who have insured the charity's nine-seater bus free of charge. "I just want them to know how grateful we are and how much we appreciate it."

But he is modest about his own contribution. "In the long, lonely journey of cancer, having a service like this up and running helps ease the burden for these people and takes another worry off their shoulders at a vulnerable time. Because as we always say, if you live in Donegal and you're diagnosed with cancer, you either travel or you die."

SHALOM CONFLICT CENTER

Shalom was founded in 2009 by Fr. Patrick Devine, SMA, a social entrepreneur and missionary priest with 25 years of experience helping to mitigate conflict and poverty in Africa. Fr. Devine is a life- long friend of Austin, our Managing Director here at Donegal Rapeseed Oil. He serves as the organization's executive director, leading an international team of conflict resolution experts from various religious backgrounds and disciplines who are based in Kenya and neighbouring countries. In 2013, he was honoured with the International Caring Award, whose previous recipients include the Dalai Lama, Bill Clinton, and Mother Teresa. We have chosen to contribute proceeds of this cookbook to Shalom to help raise awareness of this admirable charity and there tireless efforts.

In ongoing African conflict environments where people are killed, injured, and displaced, values such as peace, truth, justice, mercy and reconciliation cannot take deep root. It is very difficult to sustain development if schools, hospitals, training programs, water sources and other infrastructure are destroyed.

The organisation sets out to tackle the root causes by:

- Supporting communities to rebuild relationships that have been fractured through training peace building professionals.
- Delivering quality conflict management training to local communities and leaders.
- Working with local leaders and influential opinion shapers to ensure they are part of the long-term solution to preventing conflict.
- Promoting the construction and development of interethnic schools, medical centres, and water projects.
- Conducting Peace Education in primary and secondary schools and with groups of influential opinion shapers in conflict environments.

What are Shalom's goals?

Shalom aims to end the cycle of violence and war through peace building, human development and reconciliation. In the coming years, Shalom plans to bring its successful model of conflict resolution to other communities and countries in the region where violence continues to destabilize societies, people are unable to meet their basic human needs or fulfil their potential. Shalom is guided by the philosophy that conflicts are essentially about inadequately met human needs. The Shalom Center is driven by the need to work for positive peace, which involves breaking down barriers, including those dealing with human rights and the environment, in the belief that human needs which are not addressed eventually contribute to physical violence.

WWW.SHALOMCONFLICTCENTER.ORG

Table of Contents

STARTERS

Chicken Wings with BBQ Sauce	10
Marinated Heirloom Tomatoes	12
Creamy Wild Mushroom Tart	14
Goat Cheese with Roasted Peppers	16
Crab Meat, Lobster and Monk Liver Salad	18
Irish Albacore Tuna Carpaccio	20
Salmon Roulade	22
Thai Fishcakes	24
Sizzling Garlic Chilli Prawns	26

SALADS

Beetroot Salad with Raspberry Dressing	28
Chicken Caesar Salad	30
Chicken, Couscous and Rocket Salad with Citrusy Orange	32
Raw Beet Salad	34
Warm Bacon and Potato Salad with Honey and Mustard Dressing	36

SOUP

Butternut Squash with Coconut and Chilli Soup	38
Minestrone Soup	40
Roasted Sweet Potato and Carrot Soup	42
Creamy Tomato Soup	44
Carrot and Lentil Soup	46

MAINS

Salmon and Leek Fishcakes	48
Grilled Salmon Steaks with Hickory Smoked Butter	50
Pan Seared Cod, Garlic Potatoes and Salsa Verde	52
Cod Fillets with Lemon Chive Sauce	54
Monkfish with Curried Mussels and Chargrilled Vegetables	56
Lobster Risotto	58
Spanish Chicken Thigh and Potato Bake	60
Chicken Thighs with Sweet Potatoes	62
Hearty Donegal Chicken Casserole	64
Cream Cheese stuffed Chicken with Mushroom Fricassee	66
Hong Kong Style Chicken	68
Thai Chicken Stir Fry	70
Chicken Korma	72
Chicken Cacciatore	74
Japanese Miso Ramen	76
Turkey Burgers with Sweet Potato Fries	78
Lamb Curry	80
Irish Stew	82
Wholewheat Spaghetti Carbonara	84
Bacon and Mushroom Tagliatelle	86
Pork Chops with Sage Tagliatelle	88
Pork Belly with Apple Salad and Hickory Smoked Dressing	90
Chorizo and Salami Pizza	92

Legend

 NUMBER OF SERVES

 PREPARATION TIME

 COOKING TIME

Table of Contents

Chilli Beef Burger with Chilli Jam — 94
Chilli Con Carne — 96
Fillet of Beef with Chunky Chips — 98
Beef Fajitas — 100
Beef Lasagne — 102
The Perfect Steak — 104
Fillet Steak with Potato Millefeuille & Crispy Onion Rings — 106
Ribeye with Tomato Salsa and Smoky Paprika Potatoes — 108

BREAD AND BAKES

White Chocolate Tart with Strawberry Lavender Compote — 110
Donegal Rapeseed Oil and Elderflower Jelly, Freeze Dried Strawberries, Elderflower Sorbet — 112
Perfect Scones — 114
Irish Soda Bread — 116
Cheese and Onion Yeast Bread — 118
Brown Bread — 120
Cheese and Seed Bread — 122
Banana and Walnut Bread — 124
Raspberry, Coconut and Lemon Loaf — 126
Carrot Cake — 128
Chocolate Cake — 130
Apple and Donegal Rapeseed Oil Cake — 132
Donegal Rapeseed Oil, Orange, Rosemary and Polenta Cake — 134
Strawberry Muffins — 136

LUNCH AND LIGHT BITES

Baked Potato with Grated Cheese and Ballymaloe Relish — 138
3 Cheese Chorizo — 140
Bacon 'n' Egg Muffins — 142
Poached Egg with Sourdough Bruschetta — 144
Shakshuka — 146
Huevos Rancheros — 148

DRESSINGS AND DIPS

Hummus with Garlic, Chilli and Parmesan — 150
Crushed Chickpeas — 152
Cherry Tomato Salsa — 152
Curry and Mango Dip — 152
Guacamole — 153
Sundried Tomato Pesto — 153
Garlic Pesto — 154
Hidden Veggie Tomato Sauce — 154
Honey and Rapeseed Oil Dressing — 155

MARINADES

Garlic and Herb Marinade — 156
Steak Marinade — 156
Kebab Marinade — 156
Chicken Marinade — 157
Lamb Marinade — 157
Fish Marinade — 158
Pork Marinade — 158

Chicken Wings with BBQ Sauce

 6 SERVES   15 MINUTES   45 MINUTES

INGREDIENTS

24 large chicken wings
Donegal Rapeseed Oil infused with Garlic, for drizzling
Salt and pepper, to season
Chopped parsley, to garnish

BBQ sauce
2 tbsp Donegal Rapeseed Oil
1 onion, finely chopped
2 garlic cloves, crushed
1 tbsp brown sugar
1 tbsp mustard
125ml tomato ketchup
125ml brown sauce
2 tbsp of tomato purée
2 tbsp white wine vinegar
1 tbsp Worchester sauce
200g chopped tomatoes
Tabasco sauce
Sea salt and freshly ground pepper

PREPARATION METHOD

Preheat oven to 220°C. Line a baking tray with parchment paper.

Place all wings in a medium sized bowl. Drizzle the wings with Donegal Rapeseed Oil infused with Garlic and toss well, making sure each wing is well coated.

Sprinkle the chicken wings with the salt and pepper, and toss well.

Arrange the wings in a single layer on the prepared baking tray. Bake for about 40 to 45 minutes or until they're golden and crispy.

Sprinkle with more salt and pepper and garnish with some chopped parsley.

BBQ sauce

Fry onions and garlic in Donegal Rapeseed Oil until soft, add the rest of the ingredients and simmer for 10 minutes, until thickened.

Blitz with food processor and serve warm.

Marinated Heirloom Tomatoes

BY GREG MURPHY - THE BROOK INN
WWW.THEBROOKINN.IE

 4 SERVES   60 MINUTES   20 MINUTES

INGREDIENTS

Heirloom Tomatoes
4 large heirloom tomatoes (whatever colours you wish to use)
8 cherry heirloom tomatoes (orange and yellow)
2 sprigs thyme
8 basil leaves left whole
Donegal Rapeseed Oil
Rock salt and black pepper

Donegal Rapeseed Oil Pesto
1 basil leaf
15g toasted pine nuts
Sea salt and black pepper to taste
115ml Donegal Rapeseed Oil
10g Parmesan cheese grated
2 garlic cloves

Black Olive Dust
50g good quality black olives with stones removed

Buffalo Mozzarella
12 pieces cherry buffalo mozzarella
50ml Donegal Rapeseed Oil
1 sprig thyme
1 sprig basil leaf
Freezer bag or Sous Vide bag

Pickled Shallots
2 banana shallots
40g caster sugar
60ml white wine vinegar
Pinch of salt
1 star anise
2 cloves

PREPARATION METHOD

Buffalo Mozzarella
Place the mozzarella in a sealable freezer bag with the Donegal Rapeseed Oil, thyme and basil. Seal the bag and leave to marinate over night in the fridge.

Black Olive Dust
Remove the stones from the olives and place on a baking tray. Leave in the oven over night on its lowest setting to dehydrate the olives. Blend the olives to a fine powder and leave to one side.

Donegal Rapeseed Oil Pesto

Blitz all ingredients together in a food processor.

Pickled Shallots

Peel the banana shallots and cut into rings. You will need 16 nice rings for this recipe. Add the remaining ingredients to a saucepan. Bring to the boil and remove from the heat. Leave to cool and pour into glass jar and add the shallot rings. Leave overnight to infuse.

Heirloom Tomatoes

Place a pot of water on high heat. Cut a cross at the top of the large heirloom tomatoes. Have a bowl of iced water ready. When the pot of water comes to the boil drop the heirloom tomatoes into it for 10 seconds. Remove from the water and place into the iced water for 2 minutes. This will help the skins to come away easily. Once cooled remove the skins and cut tomatoes into desired shapes.

In a bowl add the cut heirloom tomatoes, the cherry tomatoes, the thyme, basil and Donegal Rapeseed Oil, sea salt and black pepper. Leave to marinate for fifteen minutes.

To Serve

Take half of the cherry mozzarella balls and roll them in the black olive powder. Remove the shallot rings from the pickling liquor.

Place the tomatoes in the centre of the glass plates. Drizzle with the basil pesto. Place 2 of the coated mozzarella balls and 1 of the plain mozzarella balls on top of the tomatoes.

Next place 4 shallot rings around the tomatoes and a few of the basil leaves from the tomatoes. Drizzle with more basil pesto.

Garnish with a bread stick and serve.

Creamy Wild Mushroom and Spinach Tart

 2 SERVES   5 MINUTES   15 MINUTES

INGREDIENTS

8 tbsp Donegal Rapeseed Oil infused with White Truffle
25g unsalted butter
250g mixed wild mushrooms
Sea salt and freshly ground black pepper
100g baby spinach leaves
2 shop bought, pre-baked savoury tartlet cases
Parmesan shavings, to serve

PREPARATION METHOD

Preheat your oven to 200°C or Gas Mark 6. Heat a frying pan over a high heat until hot. Once hot add 2 tbsp of the Donegal Rapeseed Oil infused with White Truffle and the butter. When the butter is foaming add the mushrooms and fry until lightly golden and soft.

Season the mushrooms with sea salt and black pepper. Add the cream and bring to the boil. Once boiled turn down to a simmer and cook for 4-5 minutes until the cream has thickened.

Add the baby spinach and cook for a further 1-2 minutes until the spinach has wilted.

Stir the remaining truffle oil through the mix, taste and season again if needed.

Spoon the mushroom mix into the tartlet cases and place into the oven for 2-3 minutes.

Serve and top with a few parmesan shavings.

Goat Cheese with Roasted Peppers

 2 SERVES   10 MINUTES   15 MINUTES

INGREDIENTS

1 red pepper, cut into a large dice
1 yellow pepper, cut into a large dice
½ courgette, thickly sliced
4 tbsp Donegal Rapeseed Oil, plus extra for drizzling
Sea salt and freshly ground black pepper
2 thick slices crusty bread
2 slices of goat cheese log

PREPARATION METHOD

Place the peppers and courgettes into a large bowl. Add the Donegal Rapeseed Oil and toss well to coat the vegetables. Season with sea salt and black pepper. Chargrill the vegetables on a hot chargrill pan. Preheat your oven to 200°C or Gas Mark 6. Brush the bread slices on both sides with Donegal Rapeseed Oil. Place the bread on a baking tray and cook in the oven for 8-9 minutes until crispy.

Place the goats' cheese slices onto the bread and place under a hot grill to brown the cheese.

Serve with the vegetables and drizzle with a little extra Donegal Rapeseed Oil.

STARTERS

Crab Meat, Lobster and Monk Liver Salad

BY SHTERYO YURUKOV - SAGE RESTAURANT
WWW.SAGEWESTPORT.IE

 2 SERVES   30 MINUTES   10 MINUTES

INGREDIENTS

150g crab meat

1 stalk celery, chopped

Small head shallot, diced

1 tbsp apple, diced

1 tbsp crème fraiche

1 tsp lemon juice

Salt and freshly ground pepper

150g Lobster Meat

Monk Liver

150g Monk Liver

1 tbsp Donegal Rapeseed Oil

1 tsp lemon juice

1 tsp Coriander

½ Red Chilli

PREPARATION METHOD

Crab Meat

Mix the ingredients all together and season them with salt and pepper.

Lobster Meat

Cook the lobster in boiling water for 5 to 8 minutes, depending on the size. Crack the shells and take out the meat. Reserve on the side.

Monk Liver

This product is underrated but it's like foie gras and you can get it from your local fishmonger. It can be marinated and pan fried or you can make a lovely parfait.
Marinate the monk liver in Donegal Rapeseed Oil, lemon juice, coriander and red chilli and pan fry.

E RESTAURANT, RUN BY CHEF SHTERYO YURUKOV AND FRONT OF
SE PARTNER EVA IVANOVA FOR THE LAST THREE YEARS, IS ONE OF THE
RIES IN THIS AREA THAT HAS GROWN QUICKLY IN POPULARITY.

N A LANDSCAPE WITH ACCESS TO SOME OF THE BEST PRODUCE IN THE
NTRY, CUSTOMERS LOVE HOW HEAD CHEF SHTERYO COOKS THEM,
LY AND RESPECTFULLY. HIS TALENT LIES IN CREATING DISHES THAT LET
FLAVOUR OF THE INGREDIENTS SPEAK FOR THEMSELVES. HE AIMS TO
 THE STANDARD HIGH AND KEEP EXPERIMENTING WITH NEW DISHES.
ARE HAPPY WHEN PEOPLE GIVE POSITIVE FEEDBACK AND RECOGNITION
S WORK" EVA SAYS.

INGREDIENTS

2 egg yolks
200ml Donegal Rapeseed Oil
1 tsp lime juice
½ tsp wasabi paste
Salt and freshly ground pepper

2 egg yolks
50ml yuzu purée
⅓ tsp Dijon mustard
⅓ tsp garlic purée
200ml Donegal Rapeseed Oil
Salt and freshly ground pepper

PREPARATION METHOD

Wasabi Mayonnaise

Put egg yolks, wasabi paste, and lime juice in mixer attached with balloon whisk. Mix at a medium speed until all ingredients are combined well. Increase the speed and start adding the Donegal Rapeseed Oil slowly until you get the right consistency. Season with salt and pepper.

Yuzu Aioli

Put egg yolks, mustard, garlic and yuzu puree in blender. At a high speed start adding the Donegal Rapeseed Oil. Season with salt and pepper.

Place the crab meat, lobster and monk liver on the plate. Squeeze on a few dots of the yuzu aioli and wasabi mayonnaise. Dress with some greens leaves and finish it with a drizzle of Donegal Rapeseed Oil infused with Fennel.

Irish Albacore Tuna Carpaccio

 2 SERVES   **30 MINUTES**   **2 MINUTES**

INGREDIENTS

50g French beans, top and tailed
½ red onion, finely sliced
150g fresh Irish Albacore tuna
Sea salt and freshly ground black pepper
1 tbsp lemon juice
6 tbsp Donegal Rapeseed Oil infused with Fennel
Parmesan shavings, to serve

PREPARATION METHOD

Wrap the tuna in cling film and place in the freezer for 30 minutes to firm up the fish.

Blanch the green beans in boiling salted water for 2 minutes then refresh in ice cold water until cold. Drain and set aside.

Mix together the green beans and sliced red onion. In a bowl mix together the lemon juice and Donegal Rapeseed Oil infused with Fennel. Season with sea salt and pepper.

Thinly slice the tuna and place on serving plates. Drizzle with a little of the lemon juice and oil mix and season with sea salt and pepper.

Top with the green beans and red onion. Finish with a few parmesan shavings and serve.

Salmon Roulade

BY THE BURREN SMOKEHOUSE
WWW.BURRENMOKEHOUSE.COM

 6 SERVES    10 MINUTES   -

INGREDIENTS

½ cup ricotta

1 tbsp flaked Atlantic Wakame

Salt and pepper

1 tbsp Donegal Rapeseed Oil

6 slices Burren Smoked Irish Salmon

PREPARATION METHOD

Beat together the ricotta, wakame, salt, pepper and Donegal Rapeseed Oil.

Wrap the mixture into slices of smoked salmon and serve as a canapé or party snack.

Bon appetite!

RECIPE DEVELOPED BY SALLY MCKENNA - WWW.GUIDES.IE

Thai Fishcakes

BY I LOVE COOKING
WWW.ILOVECOOKING.IE

 12 SERVES   **5 MINUTES**   **15 MINUTES**

INGREDIENTS

450g skinless white fish fillets (cod or haddock)
1 tbsp fish sauce
1 egg
Small bunch coriander
1 tbsp Thai red curry paste
1 red chilli, de-seeded & finely chopped
1 clove garlic, finely chopped
Thumb-size piece fresh ginger, peeled & grated
Zest & juice 1 lime
4 spring onions, finely sliced
Donegal Rapeseed Oil, for cooking

To Serve

1-2 spring onions, finely sliced
2 tbsp roughly chopped fresh coriander
1 lime, cut into wedges
Sweet chilli sauce, for dipping

PREPARATION METHOD

Place the fish into a food processor and pulse for 3-5 seconds until smooth. Add the remaining fishcake ingredients, except the spring onion and oil, and blitz until mixture is smooth. Transfer mixture out into a bowl and stir in the spring onion.

Form mixture into 12 round and flat fishcakes. You may need to squeeze out a small bit of excess liquid as you near the end of the mixture. Heat a large non-stick pan on medium high heat with a drizzle of Donegal Rapeseed Oil. Arrange half of the fishcakes in the pan, reduce heat to medium and cook for 2-3 minutes on both sides. Once cooked, remove fishcakes onto a serving plate, wipe the pan down with paper towel, then add another drizzle of oil with heat on medium high. Once oil is hot again, add the remaining fishcakes, and cook on medium heat for 2-3 minutes on both sides.

Once second batch is cooked, arrange on serving plate and garnish with spring onion and coriander. Serve with lime wedges and sweet chilli sauce for dipping.

Fishcakes can be made a day ahead of time and kept in an airtight container in the fridge.

Chilli Garlic Sizzling Prawns

DAVIS'S RESTAURANT @ YEATS TAVERN
WWW.YEATSTAVERNRESTAURANT.COM

STARTERS

 4 SERVES   5 MINUTES   10 MINUTES

INGREDIENTS

8 tbsp Donegal Rapeseed Oil

4 garlic cloves, thinly sliced

1 small red chilli, chopped

8 cherry vine tomatoes, halved

1 kg king prawns, tails on

1 pinch salt

¼ tsp paprika

3 tbsp white wine

2 tsp flat leaf parsley, chopped

Juice from ¼ lemon

PREPARATION METHOD

Peel prawns but leave tails on and season with salt. Pour Donegal Rapeseed Oil into small frying pan and heat until foaming over medium heat.

Add chilli, garlic, cherry tomatoes & wine and sauté lightly for 2 minutes. Toss in the prawns and cook for 4 to 5 minutes, until they change colour and turn pink. Add a squeeze of lemon juice and parsley and sprinkle with paprika.

Pour into a hot terracotta bowl and serve with warm crusty bread and lemon wedges.

DAVIS'S RESTAURANT AT YEATS TAVERN IS OWNED BY THE DAVIS FAMILY FOR OVER THIRTY FIVE YEARS. THE DAVIS FAMILY WHO HAVE A PASSION FOR SERVING FRESH LOCALLY SOURCED FOOD, PRIDE THEMSELVES ON OFFERING A WARM WELCOME, AWARD WINNING FOOD, IN A BEAUTIFULLY DECORATED MODERN RESTAURANT. PROFESSIONAL FRIENDLY SERVICE WITH BOTH QUALITY AND AFFORDABILITY HAS DESERVEDLY EARNED DAVIS'S THE REPUTATION AS SLIGO'S MOST POPULAR RESTAURANT BOTH FOR LOCALS AND TOURISTS ALIKE.

Beetroot and Goats Cheese Salad with Raspberry Dressing

BY YAHI CAFÉ

 2 SERVES   10 MINUTES   -

INGREDIENTS

500g cooked diced beetroot
50g rocket
40g Fivemiletown goats' cheese
8g pumpkin seeds

Raspberry Dressing

90ml Donegal Rapeseed Oil
80g raspberries
1tsp French mustard
1 garlic clove minced
Juice of 1 lemon
Pinch of salt

PREPARATION METHOD

Prepare the dressing using a blender. Mix the Donegal Rapeseed Oil, raspberries, garlic, mustard, lemon juice & salt. Blend until smooth and transfer into a jam jar.

In a big bowl mix the beetroot, rocket & pumpkin seeds. Add the dressing to the salad and half of the cheese and mix.

Divide onto two plates and add the rest of the goats' cheese and drizzle some Donegal Rapeseed Oil on top. Serve immediately.

A quirky but stylish café serving good, wholesome & nutritious food in the mall beside Belfast's main bus station. They've hunted & gathered the very best fresh produce from local suppliers to create a menu Northern Ireland can be proud of.

Chef Rotsen heads up the kitchen, where almost everything is prepared from scratch - for the rest; they've sourced local experts to deliver fresh to the door!

All our house dressings for salads are made using Donegal Rapeseed Oil, changing monthly to match our seasonal salads.

Chicken Caesar Salad

 4 SERVES   15 MINUTES   10 MINUTES

INGREDIENTS

4 thick slices crusty white bread
3 tbsp Donegal Rapeseed Oil infused with Garlic
2 chicken breasts
1 large romaine lettuce

Dressing

1 garlic clove
2 anchovies, from a tin
Handful Parmesan cheese, for grating and serving
5 tbsp mayonnaise
1 tbsp white wine vinegar
Salt and pepper, to taste

PREPARATION METHOD

Heat oven to 200°C or Gas Mark 6. Cut the bread into cubes with a bread knife. Spread over a large baking tray and sprinkle over 2 tbsp Donegal Rapeseed Oil infused with Garlic. Rub the oil into the bread and season with salt. Bake for 8-10 minutes, turning the croutons a few times during cooking so they brown evenly.

Rub chicken breasts with the remaining oil and season. Place pan over a medium heat for 1 minute until hot. Put the chicken breasts on the pan and leave for 4 minutes. Turn the chicken, then cook for a further 4 minutes or until the juices run clear.

Crush the garlic cloves. Mash the anchovies with a fork against the side of a bowl. Grate a handful of cheese and mix with the rest of the dressing ingredients. Season to taste.

Tear lettuce into large pieces and put in a large salad bowl. Add the diced chicken and scatter half over the leaves, along with half the croutons. Add most of the dressing and toss. Scatter on the rest of the chicken and croutons, then drizzle with the remaining dressing. Sprinkle the Parmesan on top and serve.

Chicken, Couscous and Rocket Salad

BY DROP CHEF
WWW.DROPCHEF.COM

 2 SERVES   15 MINUTES   30 MINUTES

INGREDIENTS

2 chicken fillets
1 chicken stock cube
100g couscous
1 red chilli
5g fresh coriander
1 lime
1 orange
60g rocket

Dressing Mix
10g Donegal Rapeseed Oil
5g balsamic vinegar

PREPARATION METHOD

Preheat the oven to 220°C.
Heat some Donegal Rapeseed Oil in a small pan and season the chicken fillets with salt and pepper. Add the chicken to the pan and fry for two minutes on each side. Then transfer to the oven and roast for 10-12 minutes, or until cooked through and the juices run clear.
While the chicken is in the oven, dissolve the stock cube in about 200ml of boiling water. Add the couscous into a bowl. Then pour the boiling stock into the couscous. There should be about twice as much liquid as couscous. Cover the bowl with cling film and allow to stand for 5 minutes.
Chop the chilli and discard the seeds. Chop the fresh coriander. Cut the lime into wedges. Add the chopped chilli, coriander and some lime juice to the couscous and mix through.
Remove the skin from the orange and cut it into segments.
Place the cooked chicken, rocket, orange and couscous in a large bowl and mix together. Add the Donegal Rapeseed Oil and balsamic vinegar dressing to taste.

Raw Beet Salad

BY GARY STAFFORD - LYONS CAFÉ
WWW.LYONSCAFE.COM

 4 SERVES   10 MINUTES   -

INGREDIENTS

1 kg whole beetroot, washed and peeled
200ml Donegal Rapeseed Oil
½ tbsp Dijon mustard
2 tbsp honey
1 tbsp lemon juice
Sea salt and ground black pepper
Mixed seeds to garnish – pumpkin, sunflower, sesame

PREPARATION METHOD

Using a mandoline or hand grater, coarsely grate beet into matchsticks.

Combine remaining ingredients except for salt and pepper by whisking together in a bowl until you have a smooth, golden dressing.

In a large bowl, mix together the shredded beetroot and dressing until well combined and garnish with the seeds of your choice.

Warm Bacon and Potato Salad

 4-6 SERVES   10 MINUTES   35 MINUTES

INGREDIENTS

2 pounds red potatoes, quartered
2 tbsp Donegal Rapeseed Oil
8 oz bacon, chopped into small pieces
1 clove garlic, minced
½ red onion, chopped
1 stalk green onion, chopped
Salt and pepper, to season
Donegal Rapeseed Oil Honey and Mustard Dressing, for drizzling

PREPARATION METHOD

Preheat the oven to 180°C or Gas Mark 4. On a baking sheet, toss the potatoes in Donegal Rapeseed Oil. Roast for 25 minutes or until tip of knife pierces potato easily. Heat a skillet on medium heat. Add the bacon and cook for 2 minutes. Then add in the garlic and the red onion.

Sauté for an additional 3 minutes until the bacon is crisp. Put the bacon, garlic and onions, including all of the bacon drippings, into a large bowl. Add in the roasted potatoes and the green onions.

Season with salt and pepper and toss gently. Drizzle with Donegal Rapeseed Oil Honey and Mustard Dressing and serve immediately.

Butternut Squash with Coconut and Chilli Soup

BY EIMEAR O'DONNELL

 4 SERVES   15 MINUTES   30 MINUTES

INGREDIENTS

4 tbsp Donegal Rapeseed Oil infused with Chilli
1 onion, finely diced
2 cloves garlic, finely sliced
1 chilli, finely sliced
1 tbsp freshly grated ginger
1 can of creamed coconut
2 celery stalks, finely diced
1 butternut squash, peeled and diced
750ml vegetable stock
Sea salt and black pepper, to season

PREPARATION METHOD

Lightly heat the Donegal Rapeseed Oil infused with Chilli in a deep saucepan until hot.
Add the onion, garlic, chilli and ginger and simmer until the onions are soft and transparent.
Add the creamed coconut and whisk to incorporate all the flavours.
Allow to simmer for a further 5 minutes before adding the remaining ingredients as well as the stock.
Cook over a medium heat until the squash is soft.
Blend and season to taste.

EIMEAR'S PASSION FOR FOOD LED HER TO A CAREER IN THE FOOD INDUSTRY. STUDYING A DEGREE IN FOOD SCIENCE FROM UNIVERSITY COLLEGE DUBLIN, EIMEAR HAS WORKED AS AN ANALYST IN THE FOOD SAFETY AUTHORITY OF IRELAND AND IS CURRENTLY WORKING AS A MARKETING SPECIALIST FOR KERRY, THE TASTE AND NUTRITION COMPANY.

HER LOVE FOR QUALITY INGREDIENTS AND INTEREST IN NUTRITIONAL SCIENCE CAME FROM GROWING UP IN A HOME SURROUNDED BY HOME GROWN, HOMEMADE FOOD.

Minestrone Soup

BY I LOVE COOKING
WWW.ILOVECOOKING.IE

6 SERVES **5 MINUTES** **35 MINUTES**

INGREDIENTS

1 tbsp Donegal Rapeseed Oil

3-4 medium carrots, roughly chopped

3-4 celery stalks with leaves, roughly chopped

1 large onion, roughly chopped

2 cloves garlic, minced

2 litres vegetable stock

1x 400g tin chopped tomatoes

200g spaghetti

2 tbsp tomato purée

1 x 400g tin cannellini beans, drained & rinsed

¼ head Savoy cabbage, shredded

Salt and pepper

PREPARATION METHOD

Place a large pot over medium heat and pour in the Donegal Rapeseed Oil. Once the oil has heated, add the vegetables and cook until the onion has softened, about 10 minutes, stirring occasionally. Add the garlic and cook for a further minute.

Add the stock, tin of tomato and the purée and stir to combine. Season with a bit of salt and pepper. Cover pot with a lid, increase heat to medium high and bring to a boil. Once boiling, reduce heat to medium low and leave soup to simmer for about 15 minutes.

Add the rinsed beans and spaghetti pieces. Stir to mix, then cook for a further 10 minutes. Add the shredded cabbage and cook for a further 2-3 minutes, until the spaghetti is cooked.

Check for seasoning and add more salt and pepper if needed. If you prefer a thicker soup, leave to simmer until soup has thickened, or add a bit of water to thin it out if needed.

Serve while hot with slices of crusty bread smeared with salted butter.

Soup will keep for up to 3-4 days in the fridge, and can be frozen for up to 4-5 months.

- 41 -

Roasted Sweet Potato and Carrot Soup

4 SERVES   **15** MINUTES   **35** MINUTES

INGREDIENTS

500g sweet potatoes, peeled and cut into chunks

300g carrots, peeled and cut into chunks

3 tbsp Donegal Rapeseed Oil

2 onions, finely chopped

2 garlic cloves, crushed

1 litre vegetable stock

100ml crème fraiche, plus extra to serve

PREPARATION METHOD

Preheat oven to 220°C or Gas Mark 7 and put the sweet potatoes and carrots into a large roasting tin, drizzled with 2 tbsp Donegal Rapeseed Oil and plenty of seasoning. Roast the vegetables in the oven for 25-30 minutes or until tender.

Meanwhile, put the remaining 1 tbsp Donegal Rapeseed Oil in a large saucepan and fry the onion over a medium heat for about 10 minutes until softened. Add the garlic and stir for 1 minute before adding the vegetable stock. Simmer for 5-10 minutes until the onions are very soft, then set aside.

Once the roasted vegetables are done, leave to cool a little, then transfer to the saucepan and use a hand blender to blend until smooth. Stir in the crème fraiche, a little more seasoning and reheat until hot. Serve in soup bowls topped with a swirl of crème fraiche and a sprinkle of black pepper.

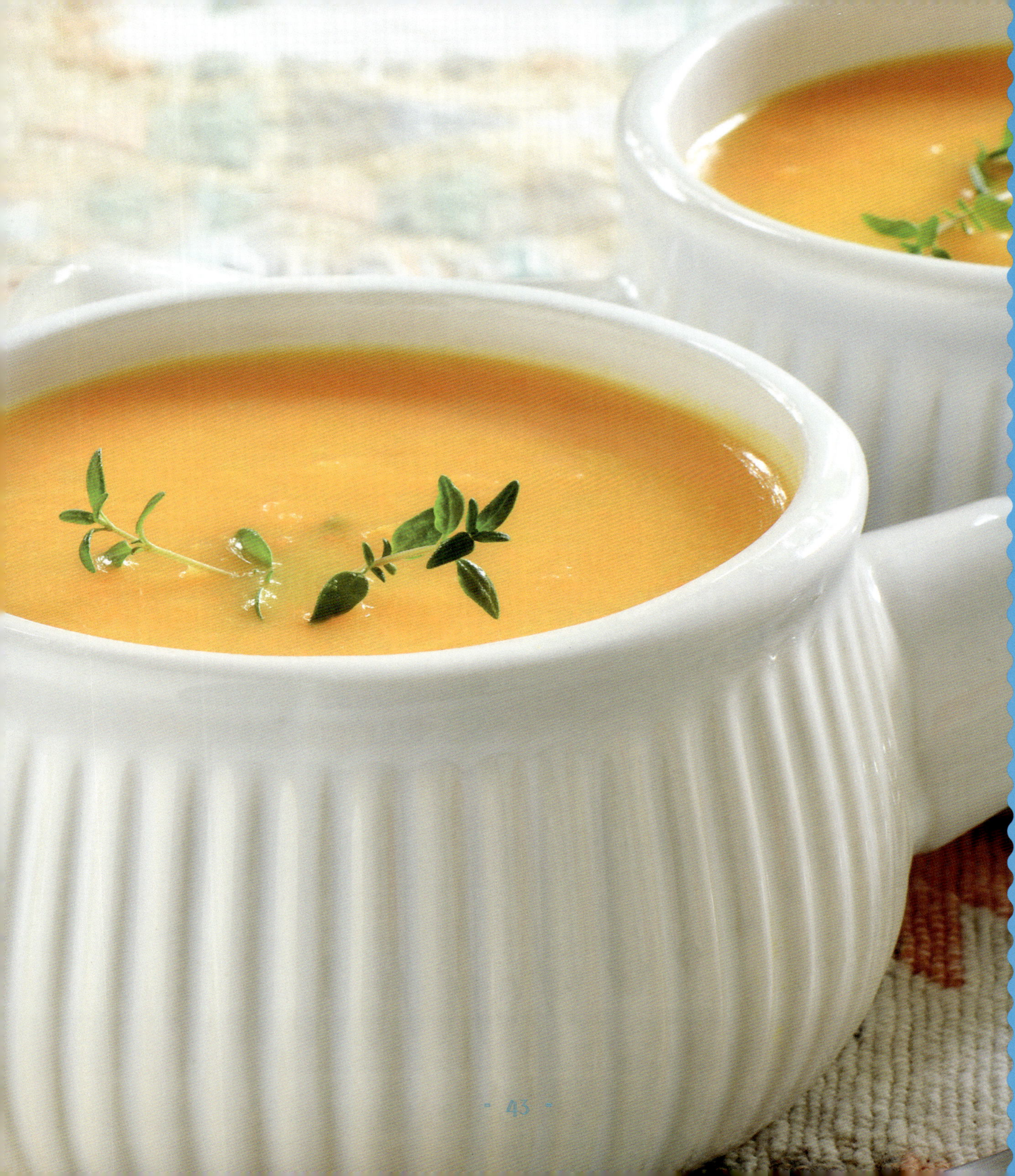

Creamy Tomato Soup

6 SERVES   **30** MINUTES   **45** MINUTES

INGREDIENTS

3 tbsp Donegal Rapeseed Oil

2 onions, chopped

2 celery sticks, chopped

300g carrots, chopped

500g potato, diced

4 bay leaves

5 tbsp tomato puree

2 tbsp sugar

2 tbsp white wine vinegar

4 x 400g tins chopped tomatoes

500g passata

3 vegetable stock cubes

400ml milk

1 litre of boiling water

PREPARATION METHOD

Put the Donegal Rapeseed Oil, onions, celery, carrots, potatoes and bay leaves in a big casserole dish, or two saucepans. Fry gently until the onions are softened, about 10-15 minutes. Fill the kettle and boil it.

Stir in the tomato purée, sugar, vinegar, chopped tomatoes and passata, then crumble in the stock cubes. Add 1 litre boiling water and bring to a simmer. Cover and simmer for 15 minutes until the potato is tender, then remove the bay leaves. Purée with a stick blender until very smooth. Season to taste and add a pinch more sugar if it needs it. The soup can now be cooled and chilled for up to 2 days, or frozen for up to 3 months.

To serve, reheat the soup, stirring in the milk, trying not to let it boil.

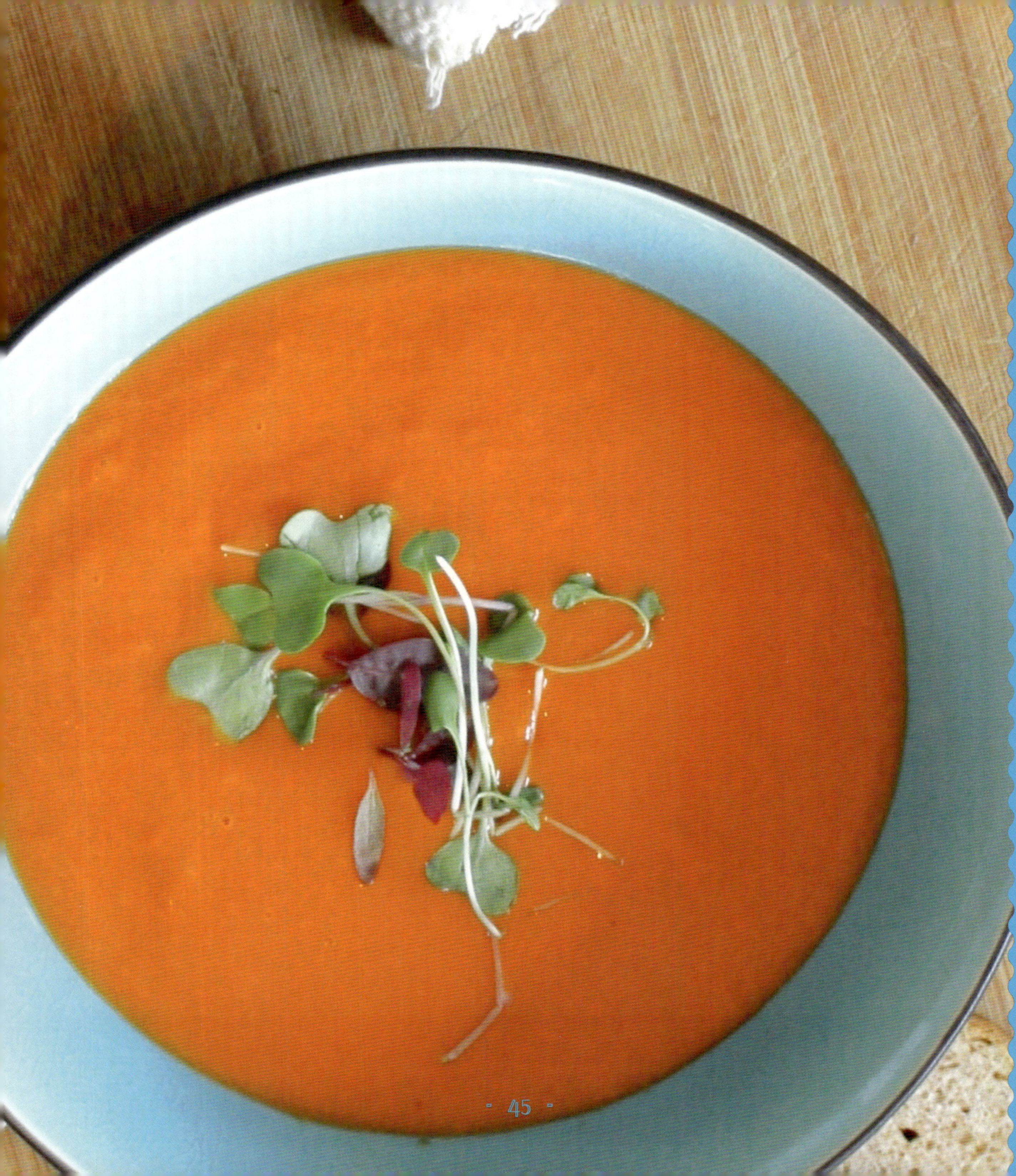

Spiced Carrot and Lentil Soup

4 SERVES   **10 MINUTES**   **15 MINUTES**

INGREDIENTS

600g carrots, washed and grated

140g split red lentils

2 tsp cumin seeds

Pinch chilli flakes

2 tbsp Donegal Rapeseed Oil

1 litre hot vegetable stock, from a stock cube is perfect

125ml milk

Naan bread and plain yogurt, to serve

PREPARATION METHOD

Heat a large saucepan and dry fry the cumin seeds and chilli flakes for 1 minute, or until they start to jump around the pan and release their aromas. Scoop out about half of the seeds with a spoon and set aside.

Add the Donegal Rapeseed Oil, carrot, lentils, stock and milk to the pan and bring to the boil. Simmer for 15 minutes until the lentils have swollen and softened.

Whizz the soup with a stick blender or in a food processor until smooth.

Season to taste and finish with a dollop of yogurt and a sprinkling of the reserved toasted spices.

Serve with warmed naan bread.

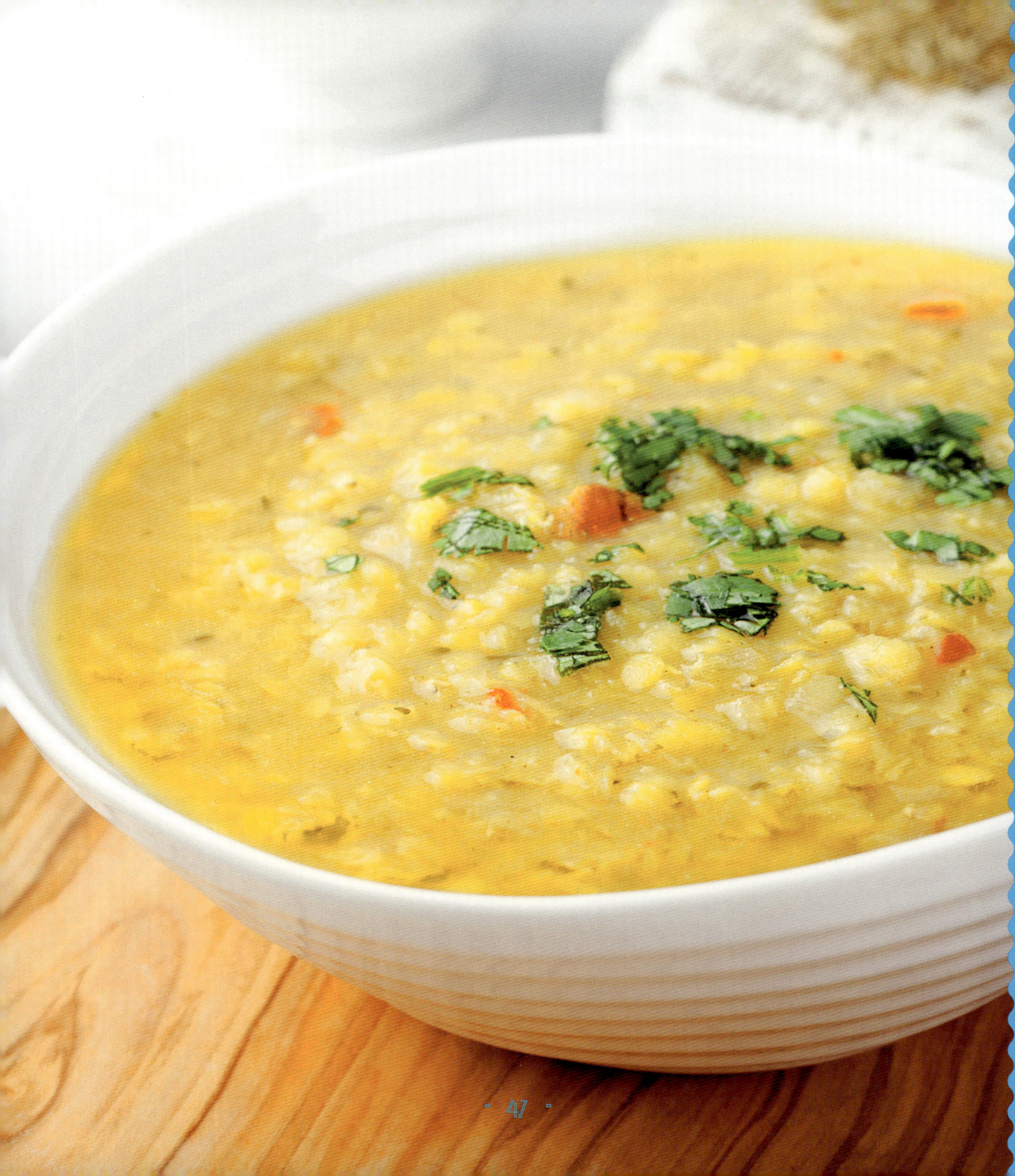

Salmon and Leek Fishcakes

BY CHRISTOPHER MOLLOY - THE LEMON TREE
WWW.THELEMONTREERESTAURANT.COM

6 SERVES   **40 MINUTES**   **30 MINUTES**

INGREDIENTS

Salmon and Leek Fishcakes

250g dry mashed potato

150g haven turf smoked salmon from Carrigart

1 tbsp chopped dill

2 tbsp chopped parsley

1 leek (half for fishcake mix, half for serving)

1 tbsp chopped capers

1 tbsp truffle mayonnaise

Donegal sea salt

Donegal Rapeseed Oil

Donegal Rapeseed Oil infused with Lemon

50g breadcrumbs

50g flour

7 eggs (1 for egg wash, 6 for serving)

100ml milk

Truffle Mayonnaise

2 tbsp chopped chive

200g mayonnaise

50g Donegal Rapeseed Oil infused with White Truffle

Parsley Sauce

500g parsley

Truffle Chips

6 large baker potatoes, from Ballyholey Farm

Parmesan cheese

Drizzle of Donegal Rapeseed Oil infused with White Truffle

PREPARATION METHOD

In a bowl mix the mashed potato, chopped salmon, leek, mayonnaise, all the herbs and cap[ers]. Season with salt and a little drizzle of Donegal Rapeseed Oil infused with Lemon.

Shape the mixture into 6 even fishcakes and place in the fridge.

In a bowl, beat the egg and milk together.

Put the flour in a separate bowl and the breadcrumbs in another; you should have three bo[wls] set up ready to coat the fishcakes.

Bread the fishcake by first dipping them into the flour then the egg and milk mix and then t[he] breadcrumb. Repeat this to all 6 and put back into the fridge.

Heat a pan with Donegal Rapeseed Oil and cook each side until golden and place in the ove[n] 200°C for 10 minutes.

Use the same pan to slowly cook your soft hen eggs and set aside on kitchen paper. Use th[e] same pan again to heat the other half of the leek to serve the fishcakes on.

For the truffle mayonnaise, whisk the truffle oil into the mayonnaise then add the chopped chive and store in fridge.

For the parsley sauce, bring a pot of water to the boil, add the parsley for 30 seconds and b[lend] in a food processor. Season with sea salt. Keep warm for serving.

For the truffle chips, peel potatoes and cut into thick chips. Boil the chips in salted water for 8-10 minutes or until just soft. Drain the water and leave them until dry. Heat a fryer to 180. Cook the chips until golden brown. Drain on kitchen paper and sprinkle with sea salt.

When serving, drizzle with some truffle oil and grate over some parmesan cheese.

Serve your truffle mayonnaise on the side as a dip.

SITUATED IN THE HEART OF LETTERKENNY ON THE WILD ATLANTIC WAY SINCE ITS ESTABLISHMENT IN 1999, THIS FAMILY OPERATED RESTAURANT OFFERS AN INTIMATE, RELAXED AMBIENCE WHERE CUSTOMERS CAN EXPERIENCE CLASSICALLY INSPIRED DISHES. THE PASSION TO SOURCE LOCAL AND SUSTAINABLE PRODUCE CAN BE ENJOYED FROM FORK TO GLASS, FROM THE LOCAL GARDEN HERBS AND VEGETABLES TO THE SELECTION OF DONEGAL BREWED BEERS. THE OPEN KITCHEN ALLOWS CUSTOMERS TO OBSERVE THE CULINARY PURSUITS OF BROTHERS, THOMAS, GARY AND EURO-TOQUES CHEF, CHRISTOPHER MOLLOY.

THE PHILOSOPHY AT THE LEMON TREE IS SIMPLE; CONTEMPORARY IRISH COOKING USING LOCAL INGREDIENTS FROM IRELAND OR WHEN POSSIBLE DONEGAL. WE BELIEVE IT IS IMPORTANT TO GIVE OUR CUSTOMERS A UNIQUE TASTE OF DONEGAL. OUR EXTENSIVE WINE LIST COMPLEMENTS THE MENU PERFECTLY.

OPEN 7 NIGHTS A WEEK FROM 5PM, AN EARLY EVENING MENU OFFERS GOOD VALUE AND A FULL A LA CARTE MENU IS OFFERED 7 NIGHTS A WEEK.

Grilled Salmon Steaks with Hickory Smoked Butter

2 SERVES · **5 MINUTES** · **10 MINUTES**

INGREDIENTS

2 salmon steaks, 170g each
150g softened unsalted butter
5 tbsp Donegal Rapeseed Oil infused with Hickory
Sea salt and freshly ground black pepper
2 tbsp chopped fresh parsley

TRY SERVING THE SMOKED BUTTER ON GRILLED MEATS OR BARBECUED CORN ON THE COB.

PREPARATION METHOD

To make the butter, place the Donegal Rapeseed Oil infused with Hickory, softened butter and parsley into a mixing bowl.

Beat until smooth and season with sea salt and black pepper.

Place the butter onto a large sheet of cling film and roll tightly to form a sausage shape. Place the butter in the fridge to chill.

Heat a grill pan over a high heat until smoking hot.

Season the salmon steaks with sea salt and pepper and lightly rub each side with a little hickory smoked oil.

Grill the salmon for 3-4 minutes on both sides until cooked through.

Once cooked top the salmon with a slice or 2 of the Hickory Smoked butter and allow to lightly melt. Serve.

- 51 -

Pan Seared Cod, Garlic Potatoes and Salsa Verde

BY O'CONNORS SEAFOOD RESTAURANT, CO CORK
WWW.OCONNORSEAFOOD.COM

4 SERVES **20 MINUTES** **50 MINUTES**

INGREDIENTS

- 4 cod fillets, 200g each
- 500ml Donegal Rapeseed Oil
- 1 bunch flat leaf parsley
- 1 bunch coriander
- 2 sprigs rosemary
- 2 sprigs mint
- 2 vine tomatoes
- 100g anchovies
- 10 black pitted olives
- 6 cloves garlic
- 1 full lemon, zested and juiced
- 50g butter
- 10 potatoes, sliced very finely
- 100ml cream
- 50g grated cheddar
- Salt and pepper, to season

PREPARATION METHOD

Finely slice the potatoes and place on a tray.

Boil up the cream, adding four crushed garlic cloves, salt and pepper and whisk in the grated cheddar. Pour the mixture over the potatoes and cover with tin foil.

Bake for 40 minutes or until soft to a knife tip.

For the cod, heat up a non-stick pan with Donegal Rapeseed Oil.

Cook skin side down first, two minutes on either side and finish in the oven for a further 6 minutes.

Finish with a decent knob of butter for flavour and allow to rest for 3-4 minutes before serving. For the Salsa Verde, finely chop all the herbs into a bowl (large enough to m at the end). Finely chop the garlic and olives and add in.

Remove the seeds from the tomatoes and finely chop into the bowl.

Finely chop in 100g of anchovies, these are optional as they are very strong in flavou

Finely season with Irish Atlantic sea salt and cracked black pepper and add in the lemon juice and zest.

This salsa is more of a dressing than a salsa so the oil is important. Add in 200ml of Donegal Rapeseed Oil and mix well. Consistency should be loose.

For plating, place the garlic potato at the bottom in the centre of the plate.

Sit the fillet of cod on top.

Place a good spoonful of Salsa Verde on top of the cod and drizzle extra around the plate.

Finish with a garnish of choice and a lemon wedge.

Enjoy.

O'CONNORS SEAFOOD RESTAURANT IS SITUATED IN THE BEAUTIFUL WEST CORK TOWN OF BANTRY, RIGHT ON THE WILD ATLANTIC WAY. O'CONNORS IS RUN AND OWNED BY PATRICK KIELY ALONGSIDE HIS PARTNER AND HEAD CHEF ANN MARIE BUTLER. O'CONNORS HAS WON BEST SEAFOOD IN IRELAND 2009 AND BEST SEAFOOD RESTAURANT IN MUNSTER 2016 AND AGAIN IN 2017 BY YES CHEF MAGAZINE. IT IS THE ONLY MICHELIN GUIDE RECOMMENDED RESTAURANT IN BANTRY.

Herb and Nut Crusted Cod Fillets

BY NEVEN MAGUIRE
WWW.NEVENMAGUIRE.COM

6 SERVES | **15 MINUTES** | **30 MINUTES**

INGREDIENTS

150g (5oz) wholemeal bread

50g (2oz) shelled walnuts, roughly chopped

3 tbsp chopped fresh flat-leaf parsley

3 tbsp snipped chives

1 tbsp of Donegal Rapeseed Oil infused with Lemon

Finely grated rind of 1 orange

Pinch of freshly grated nutmeg

75g (3oz) butter

6 x 175g (6oz) cod fillets, skin on with pin-bones removed

1 egg yolk, beaten

Steamed new potatoes, to serve

Steamed sugar snap peas, to serve

Lemon Chive Sauce:

½ small onion, diced

Finely grated rind and juice of 1 large lemon

100ml (3½ fl oz) dry white wine

150ml (¼ pint) cream

1 tsp Dijon mustard

50g (2oz) butter, diced

1 tsp snipped fresh chives

Sea salt and freshly ground black pepper

PREPARATION METHOD

Preheat the oven to 200°C or Gas Mark 6. Line a baking sheet with non-stick baking paper.
Whizz the bread in a food processor to make crumbs. Mix in a bowl with the walnuts, herbs, orange rind and nutmeg. Heat the butter in a saucepan until just melted, then stir into the breadcrumb mixture. Mix well and allow to cool.

Place the cod on the lined baking sheet, skin side down, and rub the flesh with salt and pepper then drizzle with the Donegal Rapeseed Oil infused with Lemon. Brush the top of the cod with the beaten egg yolk, then press the crumbs on top to stick. Bake in the oven for 15–20 minutes, until the fish is firm and the crumbs are crisp. Meanwhile, to make the lemon chive sauce, place the onion, lemon rind and wine in a medium pan and reduce by half. Whisk in the cream and bring slowly to the boil, then reduce the liquid again by half and whisk in the lemon juice, mustard and butter. Season to taste and stir in the chives just before serving.

Serve the cod fillets on warmed plates with a spoonful of the lemon chive sauce and arrange some new potatoes and sugar snap peas to the side.

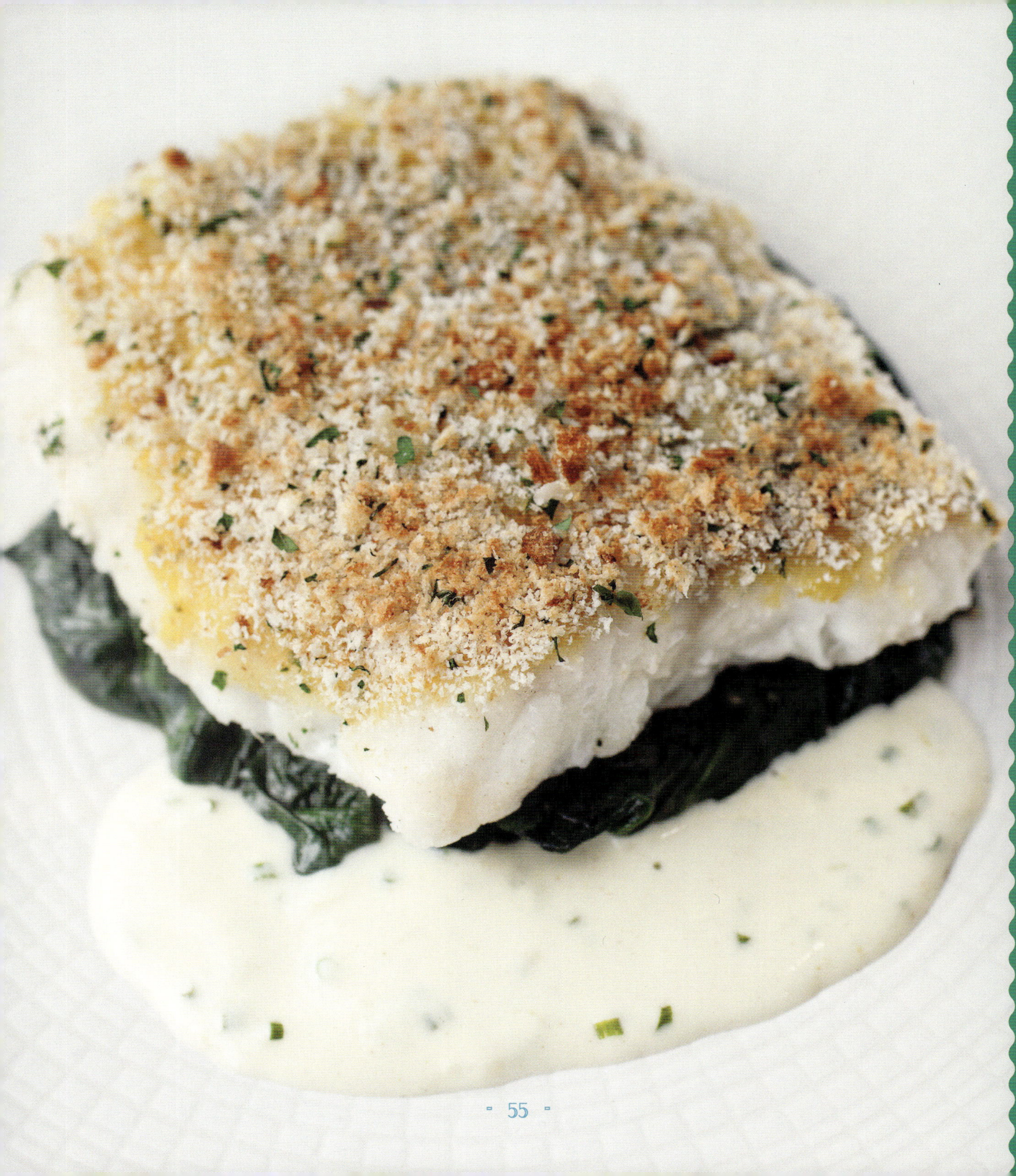

Monkfish with Curried Mussels and Chargrilled Vegetables

2 SERVES | 10 MINUTES | 20 MINUTES

INGREDIENTS

2 x 170g portions of monkfish tail
Sea salt and freshly ground black pepper
8 tbsp Donegal Rapeseed Oil infused with Curry
400g fresh mussels, cleaned
50ml cream
200g of mixed chargrilled vegetables (peppers, courgette, etc.)
Fresh dill sprigs to garnish

PREPARATION METHOD

Season the monkfish tail with sea salt and freshly ground black pepper.
Heat a non-stick frying pan over a high heat. When hot add 6 tbsp Donegal Rapeseed Oil infused with Curry to the pan.

Place the monkfish in the pan and pan fry on all sides until cooked through. Set aside.

Heat a saucepan over a high heat until smoking hot. Add the remaining curry oil. Place the mussels into the pan and cover with a tight fitting lid. Cook the mussels for 2-3 minutes until they are all fully opened. Add the cream to the pan and simmer for 1 minute. Season with sea salt and pepper.

Spoon the mussels onto a plate and drizzle over a little of the cream.

Slice the monkfish and serve with the chargrilled vegetables.

Garnish with a few dill sprigs.

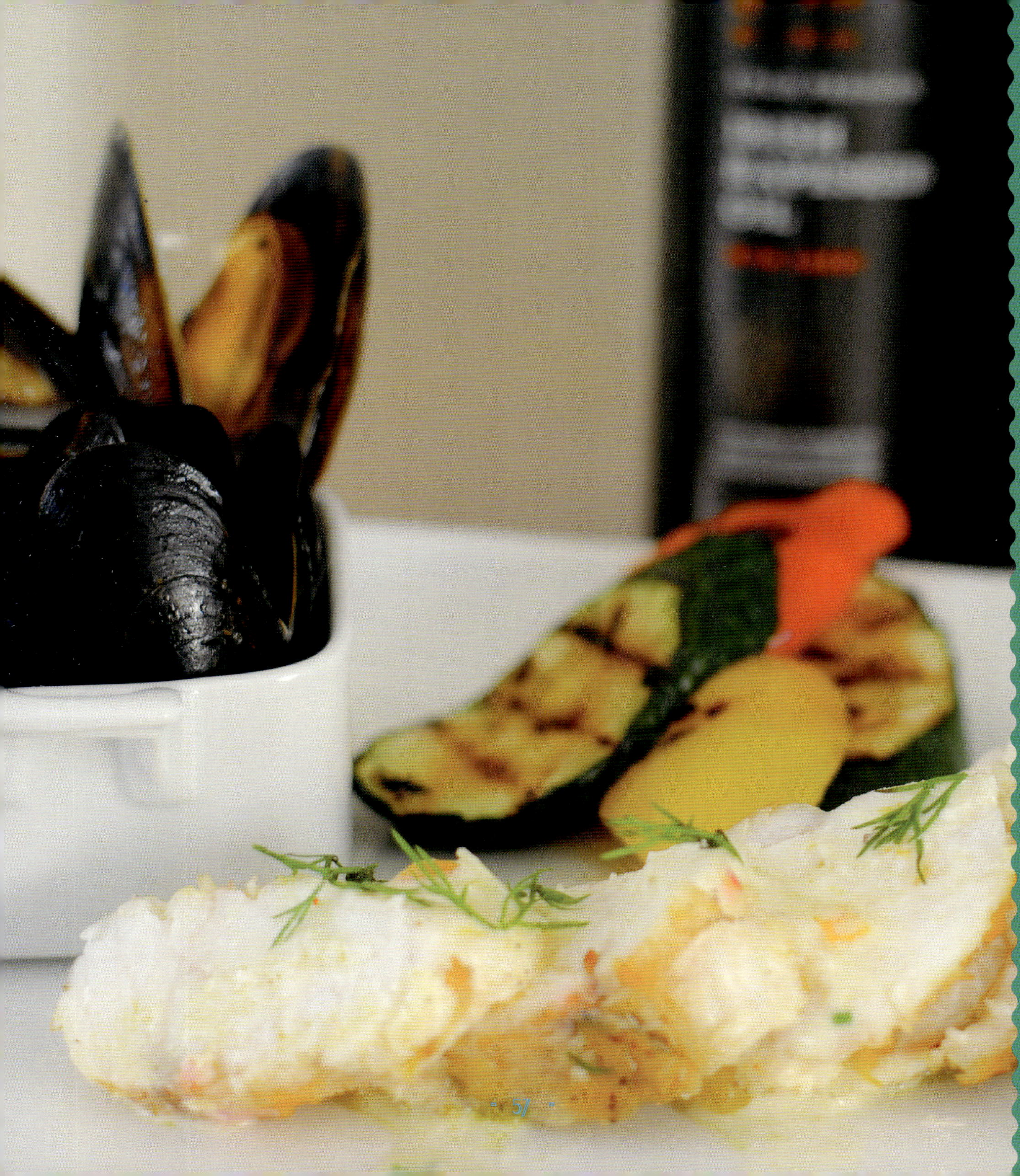

Lobster Risotto

BY THE TAVERN BAR & RESTAURANT
WWW.TAVERNMURRISK.COM

2 SERVES | 20 MINUTES | 30 MINUTES

INGREDIENTS

1 tbsp Donegal Rapeseed Oil (plus more to drizzle on finished dish)
20g butter
1 shallot, chopped
1 garlic clove, crushed
200g Arborio risotto rice
30ml white wine
About 750ml lobster stock or fish stock
200g cooked lobster meat
20g Parmesan
50ml cream

PREPARATION METHOD

In a medium pot, heat the stock.
In a large wide saucepan melt the butter with the Donegal Rapeseed Oil over a medium heat. Add the chopped shallot and garlic, and gently sauté for about 1 minute. Add the rice and the wine. Cook until the wine has absorbed.

Start adding hot stock to the rice, a cup at a time, stirring all the while, adding more stock only as the rice absorbs the previous cupful of stock. When the rice softens and becomes tender, stir in the lobster meat, Parmesan and cream.

Season to taste with sea salt and white pepper.
To finish, drizzle with Donegal Rapeseed Oil.

FOR 15 YEARS THE TAVERN MURRISK HAS BEEN THE NUMBER ONE CHOICE FOR INFORMAL DINING IN THE WESTPORT AREA. LOCATED AT THE FOOT OF CROAGH PATRICK, ON THE WILD ATLANTIC WAY, THE TAVERN IS WELL-KNOWN TO HUNGRY CLIMBERS AND LOCALS FOR SERIOUSLY GOOD FOOD AT VERY REASONABLE PRICES. IT IS RECOMMENDED BY MANY INTERNATIONAL AND IRISH FOOD CRITICS AND GUIDEBOOKS AND MICHELIN INCLUDE THE TAVERN IN THEIR PRESTIGIOUS "EATING OUT IN PUBS" GUIDE. THE TAVERN WAS SHORTLISTED FOR BEST WILD ATLANTIC WAY RESTAURANT.

MYLES O'BRIEN IS A NATIVE OF MURRISK BUT GAINED MUCH OF HIS EARLY EXPERIENCE ABROAD IN SEAFOOD AND ASIAN RESTAURANTS. THIS INTERNATIONAL EXPERIENCE INSTILLED A LOVE OF WORLD CUISINES WHICH STRONGLY INFLUENCES HIS MENUS. PROVENANCE IS IMPORTANT TO HIM AND MANY SUPPLIERS ARE NAME CHECKED, PARTICULARLY LOCAL ONES.

Spanish Chicken Thigh and Potato Bake

BY THE COUNTER DELI
WWW.THECOUNTERDELI.COM

6 SERVES **20 MINUTES** **1 HOUR**

INGREDIENTS

2 tbsp Donegal Rapeseed Oil
12 chicken thighs with skin and bone still on
750g chorizo (Gubbeen is best) whole if baby ones or cut into 4cm / 1½ inch chunks if regular sized. Please ensure it's the non-cured variety - must be raw for cooking.
1kg new potatoes, halved
Cubed butternut squash, optional
2 red onions, peeled and roughly chopped
2 tsp dried oregano
Grated zest of 1 orange
Donegal Rapeseed Oil infused with Lemon

PREPARATION METHOD

Preheat the oven to 220°C or Gas Mark 7.
Put the Donegal Rapeseed Oil in the bottom of 2 shallow roasting tins, 1 tablespoon in each. Rub the skin of the chicken in the oil, then turn skin-side up, 6 pieces in each tin.
Divide the chorizo sausages and the new potatoes between the 2 tins.

Sprinkle the onion and the oregano over, then grate the orange zest over the contents of the 2 tins.

Cook for 1 hour, but after 30 minutes, swap the top tray with the bottom tray in the oven and baste the contents with the orange-coloured juices and drizzle with the Donegal Rapeseed Oil infused with Lemon.

THE COUNTER DELI WAS BORN BACK IN 2008 WHEN RICHARD FINNEY LEFT A JOB IN A BIG FOUR ACCOUNTANCY FIRM TO PURSUE HIS DREAMS OF OWNING A FOOD AND WINE SHOP THAT HE HIMSELF WOULD LOVE TO SEE ON THE HIGH STREET. OVER THE LAST 9 YEARS THE COUNTER DELI HAS GROWN AND GROWN AND NOW ENCOMPASSES WINE, CRAFT BEER, MEATS, FARMHOUSE CHEESES, PASTAS, LOCALLY BAKED SOURDOUGH BREAD AND SPECIALITY COFFEE. JUST OVER A YEAR AGO THE SHOP DOUBLED IN SIZE WITH THE ADDITION OF A COFFEE SHOP, CULMINATING IN THE BUSINESS BEING AWARDED WINNER OF BOTH START UP OF THE YEAR 2016 AND OVERALL BUSINESS OF THE YEAR 2016 IN THE DONEGAL COUNTY ENTERPRISE AWARDS.

Chicken Thighs braised in Cider with Sweet Potatoes

BY NEVEN MAGUIRE

6-8 SERVES **15 MINUTES** **1 HOUR**

INGREDIENTS

12 rindless streaky bacon rashers
12 boneless, skinless chicken thighs
3 tbsp Donegal Rapeseed Oil
2 onions, cut into wedges
2 sweet potatoes, peeled and cut into cubes
2 garlic cloves, crushed
275g (10oz) flat mushrooms, sliced
2 tbsp redcurrant jelly
Finely grated rind of 1 orange
1 bay leaf
450ml (¾ pint) chicken stock
120ml (4fl oz) dry cider
2 tsp fresh thyme leaves
1 tbsp chopped fresh flat-leaf parsley
1 tbsp toasted flaked almonds
Sea salt and freshly ground black pepper
Creamy mashed potatoes, to serve

PREPARATION METHOD

Preheat the oven to 200°C or Gas Mark 6. Stretch each rasher with the back of a table knife, then use to wrap around a chicken thigh. Heat the Donegal Rapeseed Oil in a large casserole dish with a lid and cook the wrapped chicken thighs in batches until lightly browned all over. Arrange on a plate and set aside. Reduce the heat, then add the onions and sweet potatoes and sauté for 5 minutes, until golden. Add the garlic and cook for 1 minute, stirring to prevent the mixture from sticking.

Add the mushrooms, redcurrant jelly, orange rind and bay leaf, then pour in the stock and cider. Bring to the boil, then reduce the heat and return the chicken to the casserole and stir in the thyme. Cover and cook in the oven for 1 hour, until the chicken is completely tender and the sauce has thickened slightly. Season to taste and stir in the parsley.

To serve, sprinkle the casserole with the flaked almonds, then place directly on the table with a large bowl of creamy mashed potatoes to mop up all those delicious juices.

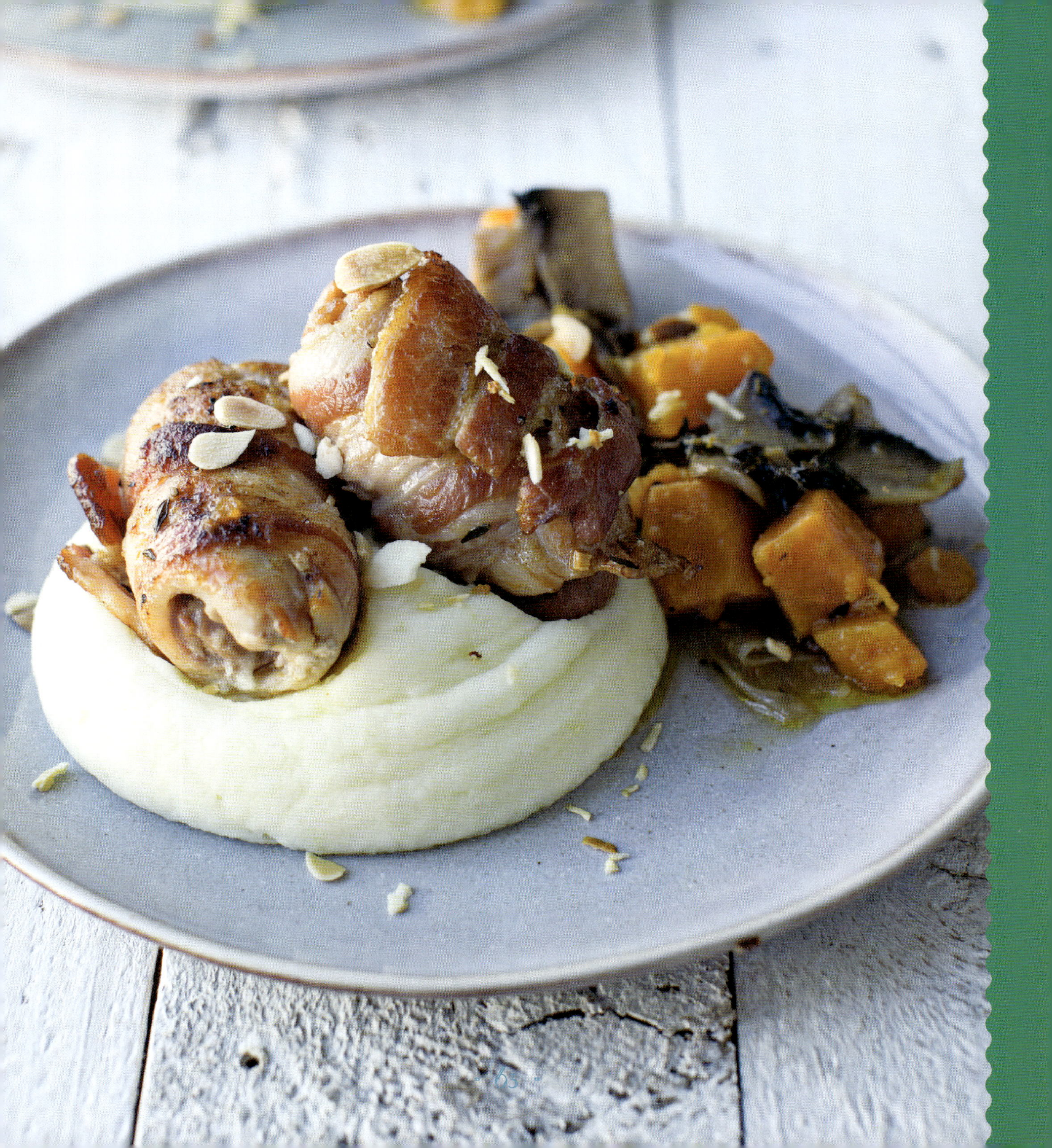

Hearty Donegal Chicken Casserole

BY BRIAN MCDERMOTT
WWW.CHEFBRIANMCDERMOTT.COM

4 SERVES **10 MINUTES** **80 MINUTES**

INGREDIENTS

400g chicken thighs

2 sprigs thyme

20g flour

2 bay leaves

25ml Donegal Rapeseed Oil

Half a leek, chopped finely

3 carrots, peeled and diced

3 parsnips, peeled and diced

2 onions, peeled and diced

2 cloves garlic, crushed

3 sweet potatoes, peeled and diced

½ litre chicken stock

25ml white wine

Fresh ground black pepper

Fresh parsley, chopped

Crème Fraiche, optional

PREPARATION METHOD

Heat a frying pan and add the Donegal Rapeseed Oil.

Coat the chicken thighs in flour and add to the pan.

Colour on all sides, season with black pepper and transfer to a casserole dish.

In the same frying pan, add and sweat the chopped onion, garlic, carrots, parsnips and leeks.

Sweat for a few minutes, then add the sprigs of thyme and white wine.

Reduce the wine slightly, add the bay leaves and warm stock.

Add the diced sweet potatoes.

Pour over the chicken in the casserole dish and transfer to a hot oven at 160°C for 1 hour.

Add Crème Fraiche, if desired, and freshly chopped parsley before serving.

Brian's Tips: Perfect dish for your slow cooker.

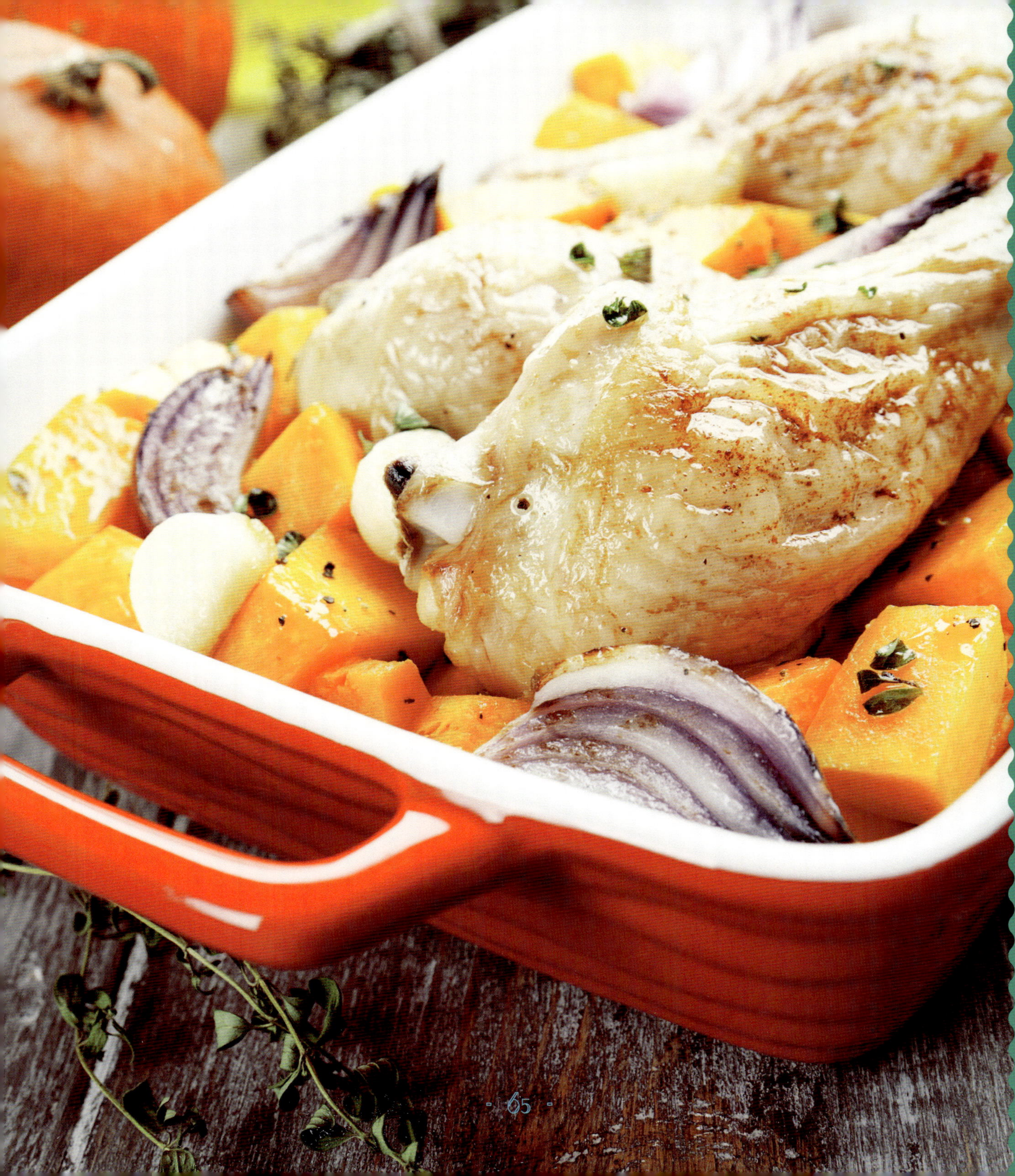

Cream Cheese stuffed Chicken with Mushroom Fricassee

2 SERVES   **10 MINUTES**   **30 MINUTES**

INGREDIENTS

2 chicken breasts, skin and wing bone on
100g cream cheese
Sea salt and freshly ground black pepper
150g button mushrooms, thinly sliced
4 shallots peeled and sliced
2 garlic cloves, finely chopped
150ml cream
100g baby spinach leaves
8 tbsp Donegal Rapeseed Oil infused with Porcini

PREPARATION METHOD

Preheat your oven to 200°C or Gas Mark 6. Season the chicken fillet with sea salt and black pepper. Make a small pocket in each chicken breast and stuff each one with the cream cheese.

Heat a frying pan over a high heat. Add 3 tbsp of the Donegal Rapeseed Oil infused with Porcini to the pan. Carefully place the chicken into the pan and sear well on each side until golden. Lay the chicken onto a roasting tray and cook in the oven for 16-18 minutes until thoroughly cooked through.

Now make the mushroom fricassee. Heat the remaining porcini oil in a frying pan. Add the mushrooms and chopped shallot and fry for 4 minutes until the mushrooms are golden in colour. Add the chopped garlic and cook for a further 1 minute. Add the cream, bring to the boil and then simmer for 3-4 minutes until thickened.

Add the baby spinach leaves to the mushrooms. Season with sea salt and pepper and cook for a further 1 minute. Set aside.

Remove the chicken from the oven and allow to rest for 4 minutes. Spoon over the mushroom fricassee and drizzle over a little more porcini oil. Serve.

Serve the mushroom fricassee on toast with salad for lunch or starter.

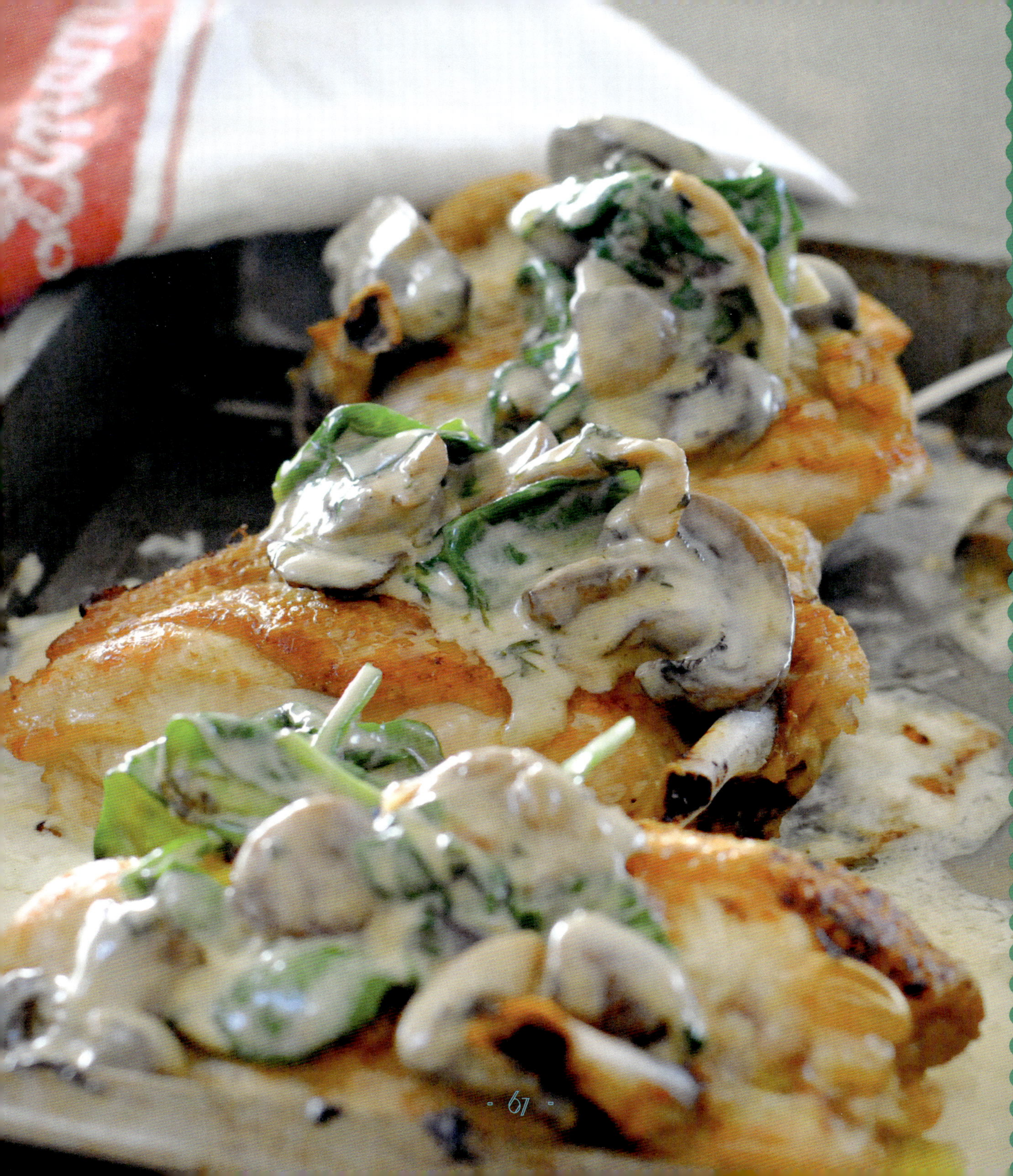

Hong Kong Style Chicken

BY KWANGHI CHAN
WWW.CHANCHANSAUCE.COM

2 SERVES | 15 MINUTES | 20 MINUTES

INGREDIENTS

2 tbsp Donegal Rapeseed Oil infused with Garlic
1 tbsp fresh ginger, grated
6 tbsp Hong Kong Street Sauce
8oz boneless chicken breast or thighs, sliced
500ml fresh chicken stock or stock cube broth
2 tbsp fish sauce
100ml coconut milk
6oz dried rice vermicelli noodles (ultra-fine)
1 lime, juiced
Donegal Rapeseed Oil infused with Lemon, for drizzling
Sliced red onion, to garnish
Red chillies, to garnish
Cilantro, to garnish
Scallions, to garnish

PREPARATION METHOD

In a large pot over medium heat, add the Donegal Rapeseed Oil infused with Garlic, ginger, and Hong Kong Street Sauce.
Fry for 3 minutes, until fragrant.
Add the chicken and cook for a of couple minutes, just until the chicken goes white.
Add the chicken broth, fish sauce, and coconut milk. Bring to a boil.
At this point, taste the broth for salt and adjust seasoning accordingly (add salt if needed, or if it's too salty, add a bit of water).
Add dried vermicelli noodles into the soup broth and cook for 4 minutes until soft.
The noodles will be ready to eat in a couple of minutes.
Divide among serving bowls, add a squeeze of lime juice and your garnishes on top, drizzle a little Donegal Rapeseed Oil infused with Lemon and a little Hong Kong Street Sauce to finish.

KWANGHI CHAN WAS BORN IN HONG KONG AND RAISED IN BUNCRANA, CO DONEGAL.
HE WENT TO TRAIN AT KILLYBEGS CATERING COLLEGE, CO DONEGAL AND ALSO GAINED A BACHELOR DEGREE IN INTERNATIONAL CULINARY ARTS FROM TVU LONDON.
KWANGHI HAS EXTENSIVE EXPERIENCE IN THE HOTEL AND RESTAURANT INDUSTRIES WORKING IN SOME OF THE TOP RESTAURANTS IN IRELAND, GAINING EXPERIENCE WITH THE BEST CHEFS IN THE COUNTRY. 2016 SEEN HIS LATEST VENTURE; CHANCHAN, PRODUCING HONG KONG STREET SAUCE AND ALSO A SPICE BAG SEASONING. THE PRODUCTS ARE SOLD IN SUPERMARKETS NATIONWIDE AND SELECTED ARTISAN FOOD STORES ACROSS THE COUNTRY.

Thai Chicken Stir Fry

2 Serves | **10 Minutes** | **10 Minutes**

INGREDIENTS

1 tsp Donegal Rapeseed Oil
2 chicken breasts, thinly sliced
2 cloves garlic, sliced
2cm fresh ginger, peeled and grated
1 red chilli, finely sliced
1 bunch spring onions, sliced
½ red pepper, seeded and cubed
½ yellow pepper, seeded and cubed
Grated rind and juice of 1 lime
1 tbsp honey
1 tbsp soy sauce
Basil
Noodle or pilaf rice, to serve

PREPARATION METHOD

Heat the Donegal Rapeseed Oil in a frying pan or wok until it begins to smoke. Add the chicken and fry for 2-3 minutes until golden. Remove from the pan and set aside.

Add the garlic, ginger and chilli and fry for 1 minute, add the spring onions and peppers and continue to fry for 2 minutes.

Return the chicken to the pan with the remaining ingredients and heat through until piping hot.

Serve with noodles or pilaf rice.

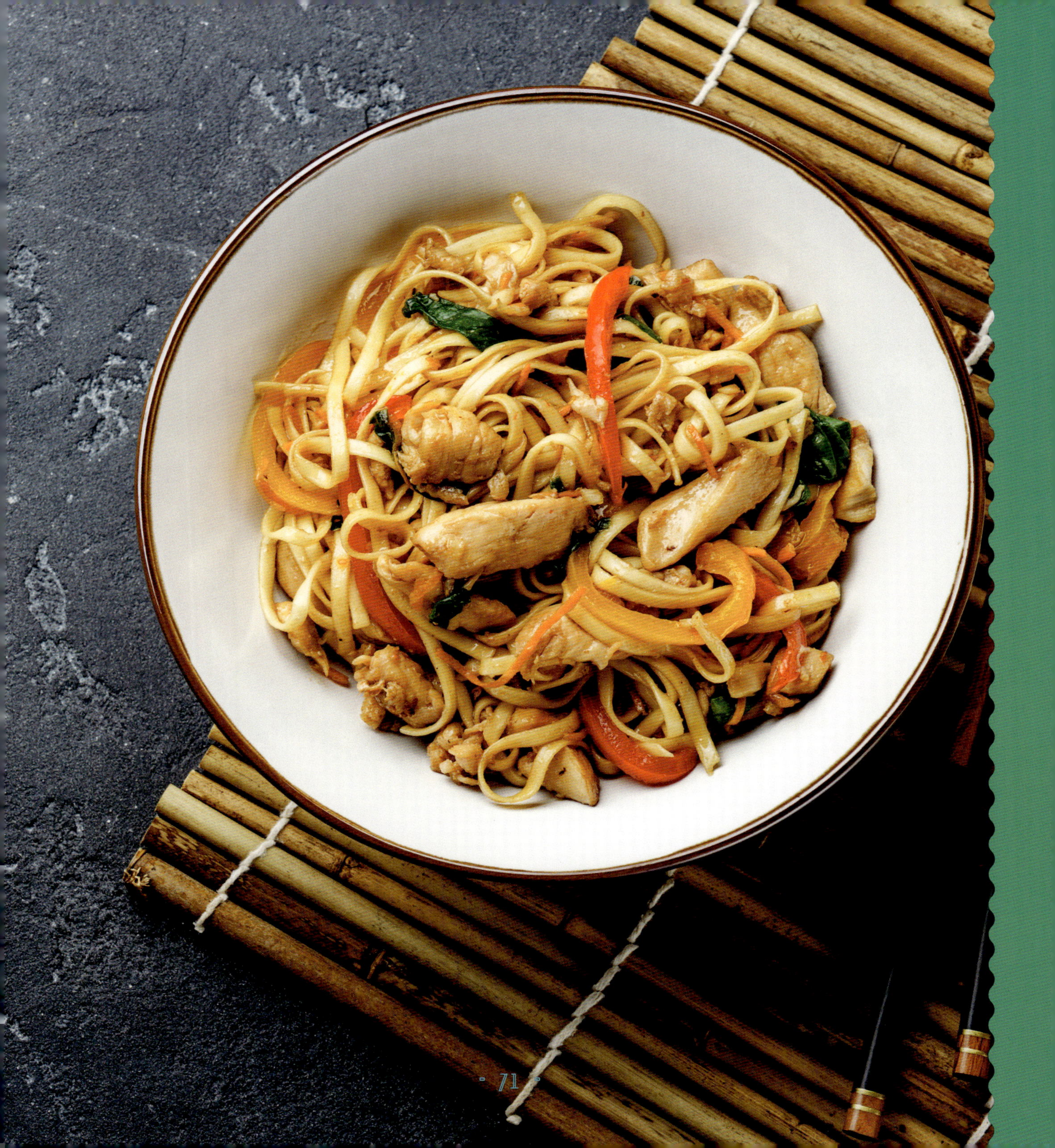

Chicken Korma

4 SERVES | **10 MINUTES** | **30 MINUTES**

INGREDIENTS

2 tbsp Donegal Rapeseed Oil
2 onions, finely chopped
2 garlic cloves, crushed
2 tsp finely grated root ginger
1 tsp garam masala
1 tsp ground turmeric
¼ tsp chilli powder
1 x 400g tin of chopped tomatoes
1 tsp tomato purée
1 x 400g tin of coconut milk
750g chicken breasts, cut into 2.5cm cubes
Sea salt and freshly ground black pepper
Steamed rice, to serve
Handful of fresh coriander sprigs, to garnish
Warmed naan bread, to serve

PREPARATION METHOD

Heat the Donegal Rapeseed Oil in a large pan set over a medium heat and fry the onions and garlic for 6–8 minutes, until golden brown. Add the ginger and cook for 1 minute, stirring.

Add the garam masala to the pan with the turmeric, chilli powder and a pinch of salt and cook for another minute, stirring. Add the tomatoes, tomato purée and 4 tablespoons of water. Stir well to combine, then bring to a fast simmer for 5 minutes, until the sauce is so well reduced that it's almost sticking to the bottom of the pan, stirring occasionally.

Stir the coconut milk into the pan, then stir in the chicken. Slowly bring to the boil, then reduce the heat and simmer gently for 10–15 minutes, until the chicken is cooked through and completely tender. Season to taste.

To serve, arrange the steamed rice and chicken korma on warmed plates and scatter over the coriander sprigs to garnish. Serve with warmed naan bread.

- 13 -

Chicken Cacciatore

BY I LOVE COOKING
WWW.ILOVECOOKING.IE

4-6 SERVES | 5 MINUTES | 40 MINUTES

INGREDIENTS

Donegal Rapeseed Oil, for cooking
4-6 chicken breasts
1 large onion, chopped
100g pancetta or smoky bacon, diced
1 punnet mushrooms, quartered
2 cloves garlic, finely chopped
150ml dry white wine
1 x 400g tin chopped tomatoes
2 rosemary sprigs
1 bay leaf
1 tsp sugar
Salt and pepper
Handful fresh parsley, roughly chopped
Soft polenta or crusty bread, to serve

PREPARATION METHOD

Heat a large lidded pan on medium high heat, then add about 3-4 tbsp Donegal Rapeseed Oil. Brown the chicken just until golden on both sides, then remove chicken from pan and set aside.

Lower heat to medium, then add pancetta and onion. Cook until soft, stirring occasionally, for about 5 minutes. Add garlic and mushrooms, cook for a further 1 minute. Add the wine and simmer for 1-2 minutes, use a spatula to scrape the brown bits off the pan.

Return the chicken to the pan, then add the chopped tomato. Sprinkle with the sugar and add the herbs. Bring to a boil, then reduce heat to medium low. Cover pot with the lid and leave to simmer for 15 minutes for smaller chicken breasts, and 20 minutes for large ones. Uncover, season with salt and pepper and increase heat to medium, then leave to cook for further 10-15 minutes until sauce has thickened.

Garnish with chopped parsley before serving on top of soft polenta or alongside crusty bread.

Leftovers will keep for up to 3 days in the fridge. To re-heat, place in pot over medium heat, add a splash of water and cover with lid. Cook until sauce is steaming and chicken is warmed through.

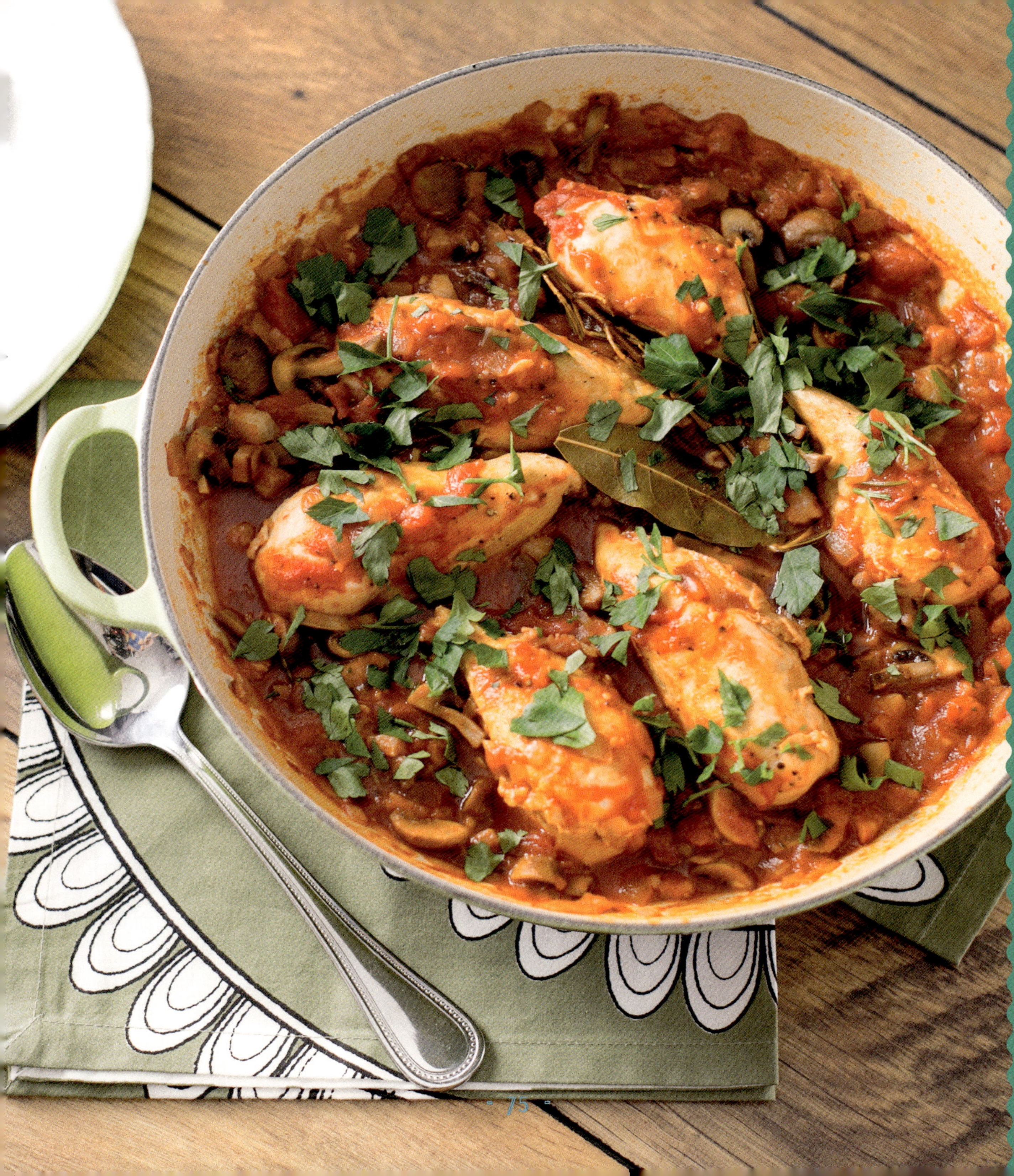

Japanese Miso Ramen

BY ETHNA REYNOLDS - NOOK CAFÉ

4 SERVES | 20 MINUTES | 30 MINUTES

INGREDIENTS

Chicken

4 free range chicken breasts

6 tbsp Sake or dry sherry

3 cloves garlic, minced

1 tbsp ginger, minced

4 tbsp soy sauce

Ramen

1 litre chicken stock

1 tbsp Donegal Rapeseed Oil infused with White Truffle

2 tbsp ginger, minced

1 tbsp garlic, minced

½ small red chilli, diced

1 tbsp soy sauce

4 tbsp white Miso paste

1 tsp sugar, level

400g Ramen noodles

Toppings

4 soft-boiled eggs

4 spring onions, sliced

½ white onion, sliced into rings

4 large mushrooms, sliced

100g bean sprouts

Pickled ginger

Selections of chillies, sliced

Coriander sprigs

Donegal Rapeseed Oil infused with Curry

PREPARATION METHOD

Mix the sake, garlic, ginger and soy sauce together and marinade chicken overnight. Pan-fry or oven bake chicken until cooked through.

Place the chicken stock into a large saucepan and add the ginger, garlic, chilli, soy, sugar & truffle oil.

Bring to the boil and immediately reduce to a simmer. Add the Miso paste and stir until it is dissolved.

Meanwhile, cook the ramen noodles in boiling water for 3 minutes, drain. Slice the chicken.

Place a good handful of noodles into the bottom of each of the 4 large bowls and top off with the broth.

Drizzle with Donegal Rapeseed Oil infused with Curry and top with the chicken along with toppings of your choice.

NOOK CAFÉ IS RUN BY AWARD WINNING CHEF, ETHNA REYNOLDS, WHO HAS TRAINED IN KILLYBEGS AND WORKED ACROSS THE WORLD TAKING INFLUENCE FROM DIFFERENT CULTURES. THE EMPHASIS IS ON LOCAL AND IRISH PRODUCE WITH A TWIST, AND A MONTHLY CHANGING SEASONAL MENU WHICH GIVES NEW FOOD PRODUCERS THE CHANCE OF BEING INCLUDED IN THE DISHES. MOST OF THE CHANGING MENUS INGREDIENTS HAIL FROM THE NORTH WEST OF IRELAND, EVEN THOUGH MANY OF THE DISHES SHE SERVES HAVE INFLUENCES FROM ALL OVER THE WORLD. NOOK OPENED IN MAY 2016, AND HAS WON NUMEROUS AWARDS, INCLUDING GEORGINA CAMPBELL'S NEWCOMER OF THE YEAR 2017.

Turkey Burgers with Sweet Potato Fries

BY I LOVE COOKING
WWW.ILOVECOOKING.IE

4 SERVES **10 MINUTES** **40 MINUTES**

INGREDIENTS

Sweet Potato Fries

2 large sweet potatoes, washed
4 tbsp Donegal Rapeseed Oil
2 tsp smoked paprika
Sea salt

Turkey Burgers

1 slice bread, crusts removed
500g turkey mince
2 spring onions, finely sliced
1 egg
½ tsp salt

To Serve (optional)

4 multigrain rolls, cut in half
Mayonnaise
Lettuce, rinsed
Tomato, sliced
Strong white cheddar

PREPARATION METHOD

Pre-heat oven to 200°C or Gas Mark 6.

For the burgers, use your fingers to rub the slice of bread into crumbs, or whiz in a food processor, then combine with the turkey mince and the rest of the ingredients in a large bowl. Use a fork to combine everything, making sure the egg is well mixed in.

Divide meat mixture into 4, then form each into a patty. You can use a burger press if you have one. Place on a plate lined with parchment paper then chill in the fridge until needed.

For the fries, peel the sweet potatoes if you prefer or you can leave the skin on, then cut sweet potatoes into fries. Place in a large bowl and add the Donegal Rapeseed Oil and smoked paprika. Toss until fries are well coated. Spread fries in a single layer onto 1 or 2 large baking sheets and scatter with sea salt flakes. Roast for 15 minutes, then gently toss or turn fries over and roast for a further 15 minutes.

When sweet potato fries have been in the oven for about 15 minutes, heat a large non-stick pan or griddle on medium high heat drizzled with a bit of Donegal Rapeseed Oil. Once hot, cook the turkey patties for 5 minutes, when golden brown, flip patties over and cook for a further 3-5 minutes until cooked through. Remove from heat.

To assemble burgers, spread about 1-2 tsp mayonnaise onto bottom half of rolls, then top with lettuce and tomato. Place a burger patty on top then finish off with sliced or grated cheddar. Position roll bun on top then serve burger with a side of piping hot sweet potato fries.

Patties can be made up to a day ahead of time. Keep chilled in the fridge in an airtight container or covered with clingfilm.

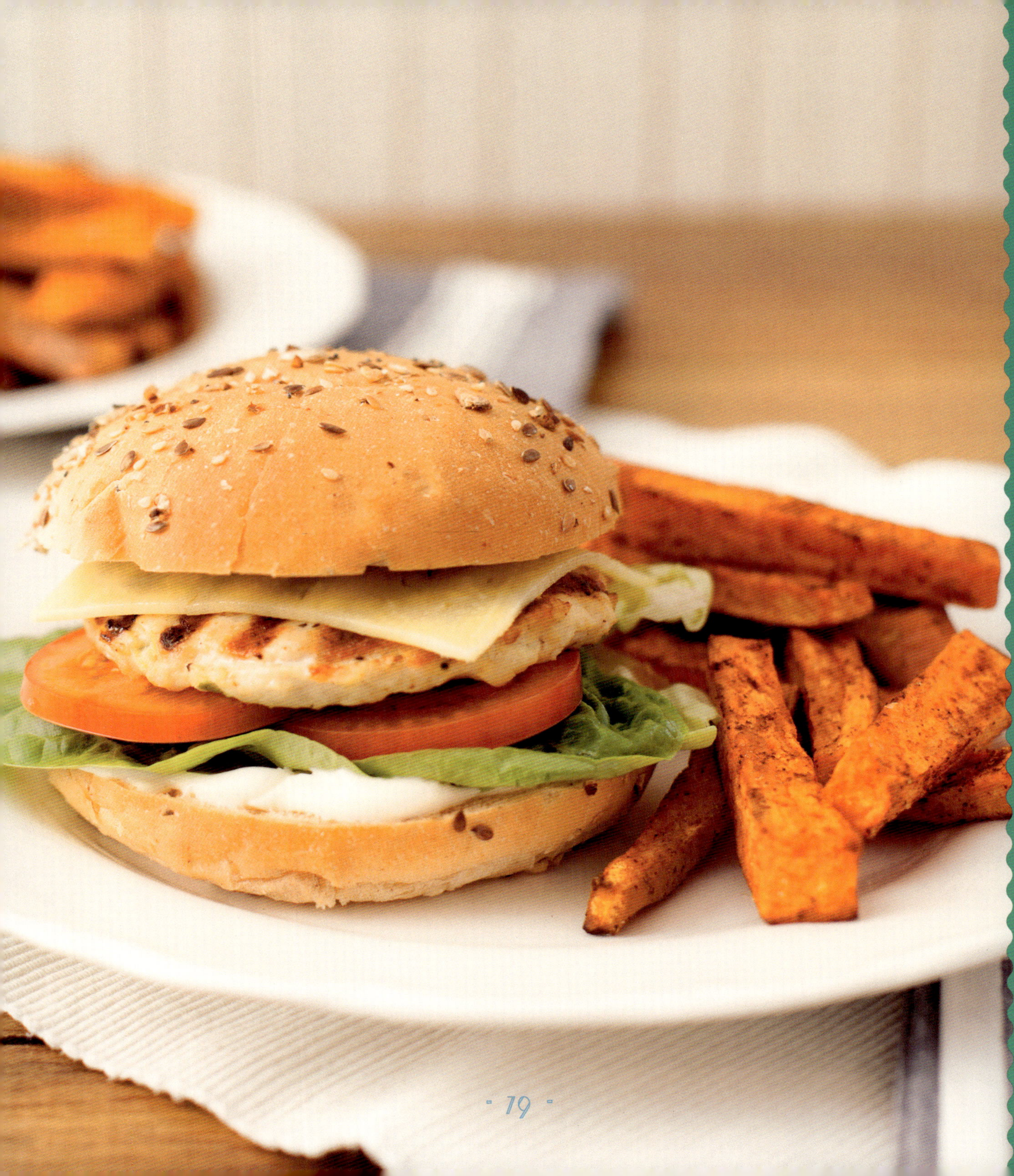

Lamb Curry

4 SERVES   **15** MINUTES   **1 HOUR 50 MINUTES**

INGREDIENTS

750g leg of lamb, diced
2 onions, quartered
4 garlic cloves
2 tbsp Donegal Rapeseed Oil
1 piece ginger, ½ into matchsticks, the rest whole
1 cinnamon stick
1 tbsp ground coriander
1 tsp ground cumin
1 tsp ground turmeric
½ tsp fennel seeds
400g can chopped tomatoes
1 red chilli, deseeded and sliced
Bunch coriander, stalks finely chopped, leaves roughly chopped
Basmati rice, to serve

PREPARATION METHOD

Put the whole piece of ginger, the onions and garlic into a food processor with 300ml of water. Blitz to a smooth purée. Scrape down the sides with a spoon and blitz again. Tip into a deep pan, cover with a lid and simmer for 15 minutes. Remove the lid and cook for 5 minutes more, stirring occasionally.

Add the Donegal Rapeseed Oil to the pan with the rest of the ginger. Turn up the heat and fry for 3 minutes, stirring until it starts to colour.

Stir in the spices and add the lamb. Stir fry until the lamb changes colour. Tip in the tomatoes with a can of water and chilli, season well, cover and leave to simmer for 1 hour.

Stir in the coriander stalks, cover and cook for a final 30 minutes until the lamb is tender. Add a small amount of water if necessary as it cooks.

Stir in the coriander leaves and serve with basmati rice.

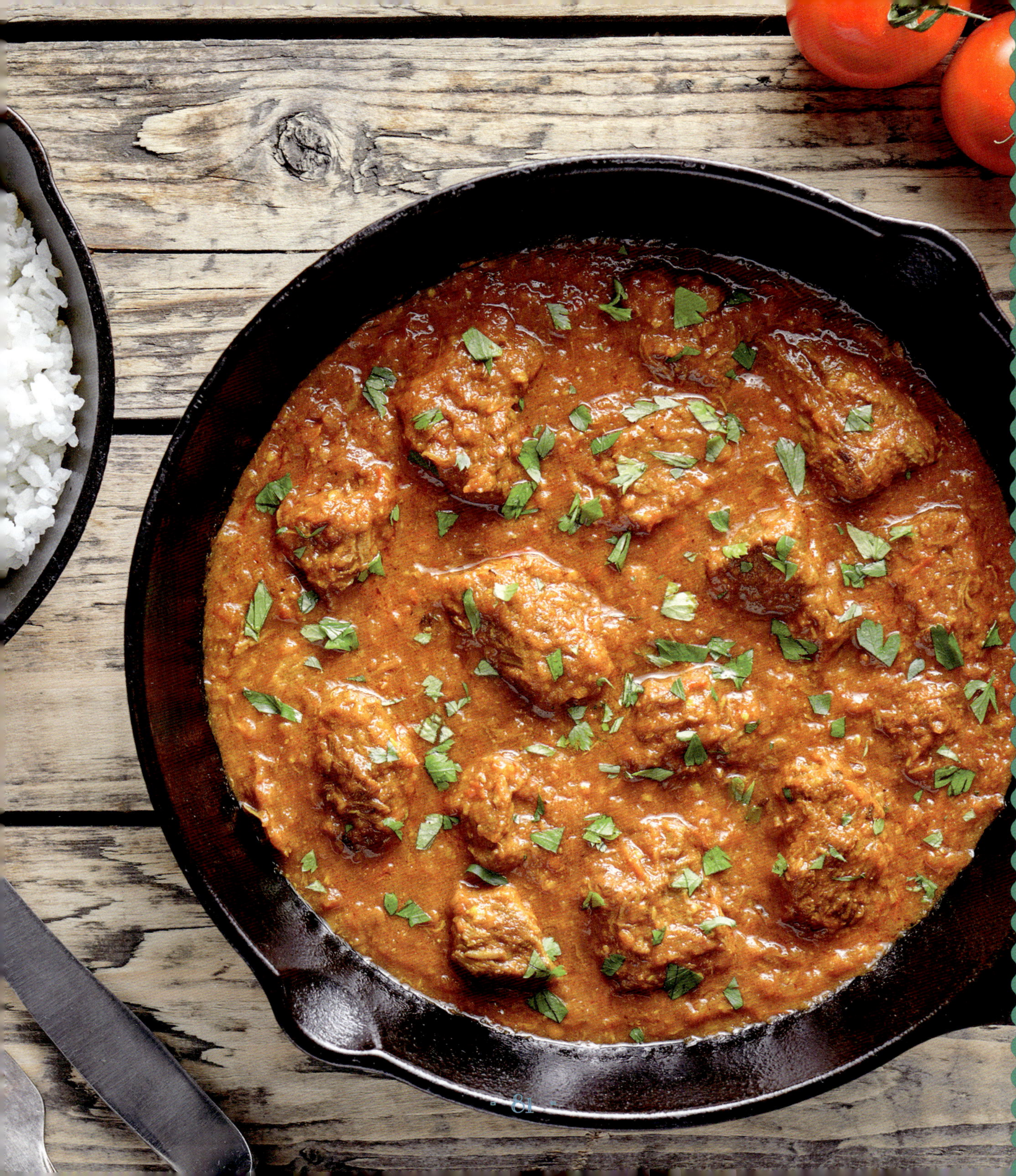

Irish Stew

4 SERVES   **30** MINUTES   **3 HOURS**

INGREDIENTS

2 medium onions, chopped

Donegal Rapeseed Oil, for frying

1 oz butter

1 sprig dried thyme

2½ lbs lamb shoulder, chopped into large pieces

7 carrots, chopped lengthways

2 tbsp pearl barley

5 cups chicken stock

Salt and freshly ground black pepper

12 medium potatoes

1 bunch parsley leaves, finely chopped

1 bunch chives

1 bouquet garni (parsley, thyme and bay leaf)

Stock

Chicken carcass

1 onion

4 cups water

3 stalks celery, chopped

Bay leaf

Salt and black pepper

PREPARATION METHOD

In a large saucepan, cook the onions in Donegal Rapeseed Oil and butter, on medium to high heat until they are translucent. Add the dried thyme and stir. Add the lamb and brown on a high heat to seal in juices. Add carrots and pearl barley. For the stock, preheat the stockpot. Combine ingredients in a large saucepan and cover with water. Bring to boil and simmer for approximately 30 minutes. Then let it cool down and skim off the fat.

Pour in the chicken stock so that it almost covers the meat and vegetables. Season with salt and pepper, and add bouquet garni. Cover and cook on low heat for 2 hours, being careful not to boil. Place potatoes on top of the stew, cover and cook for 30 minutes.

Serve the stew in large flat soup bowls, garnish with parsley and chives.

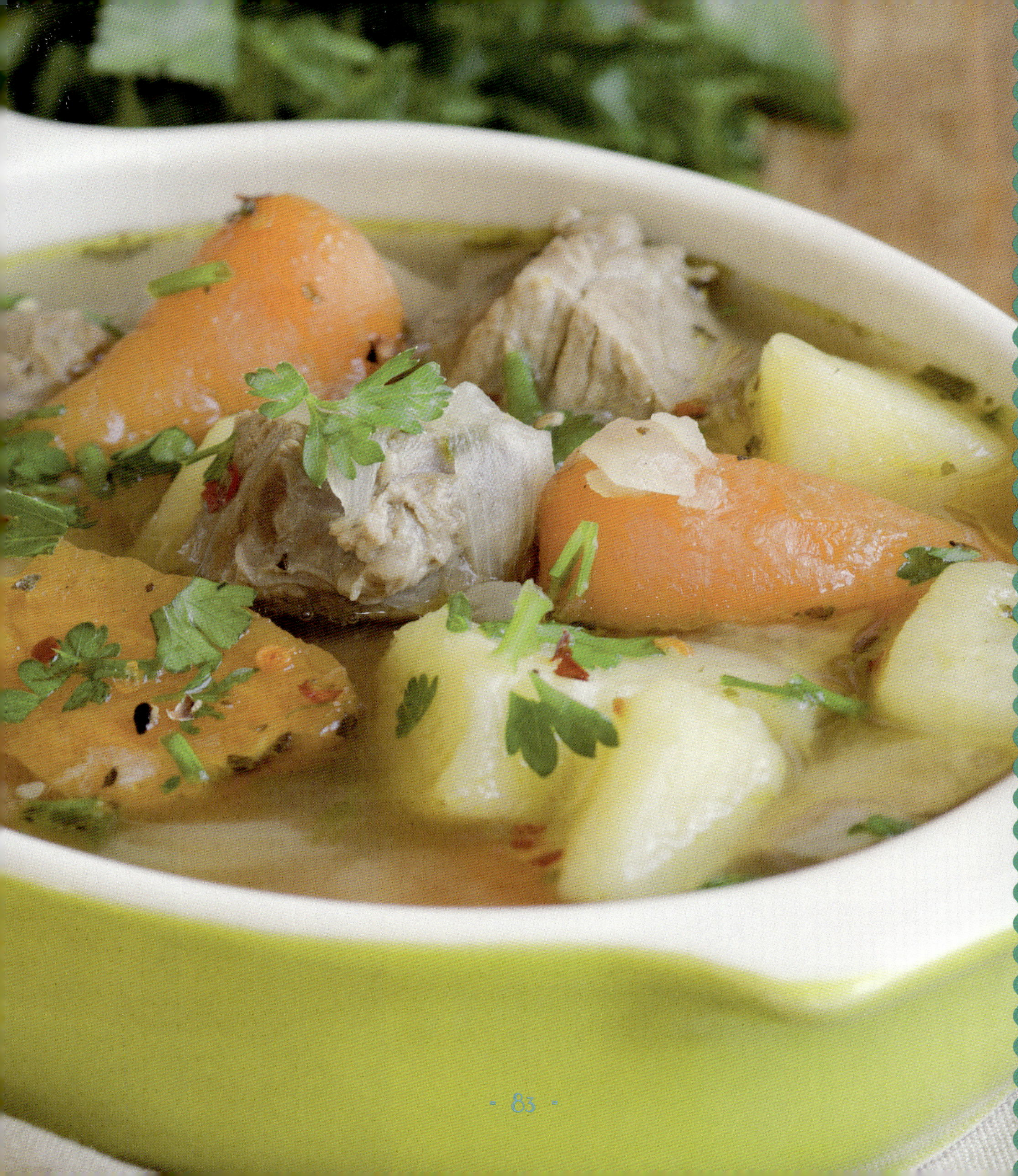

Wholewheat Spaghetti Carbonara

4 SERVES · 20 MINUTES · 10 MINUTES

INGREDIENTS

3 tbsp Donegal Rapeseed Oil
8 rashers smoked back bacon, chopped
300g whole wheat spaghetti
175g low fat soft cheese with chives
50ml semi skimmed milk
2 medium eggs, beaten
75g Parmesan, grated
1-2 tbsp chopped parsley, to serve
Mushrooms, optional
Donegal Rapeseed Oil infused with Garlic, for drizzling

PREPARATION METHOD

Heat 1 tbsp Donegal Rapeseed Oil in a frying pan and fry the bacon for 4-5 minutes until crispy.

Cook the spaghetti according to pack instructions, drain and return to the pan.

Meanwhile, mix the soft cheese and milk together, stir in the eggs, remaining oil and Parmesan and stir into the drained spaghetti, along with the bacon. Cook gently for 1-2 minutes. Serve immediately scattered with the chopped parsley and a drizzle of Donegal Rapeseed Oil infused with Garlic.

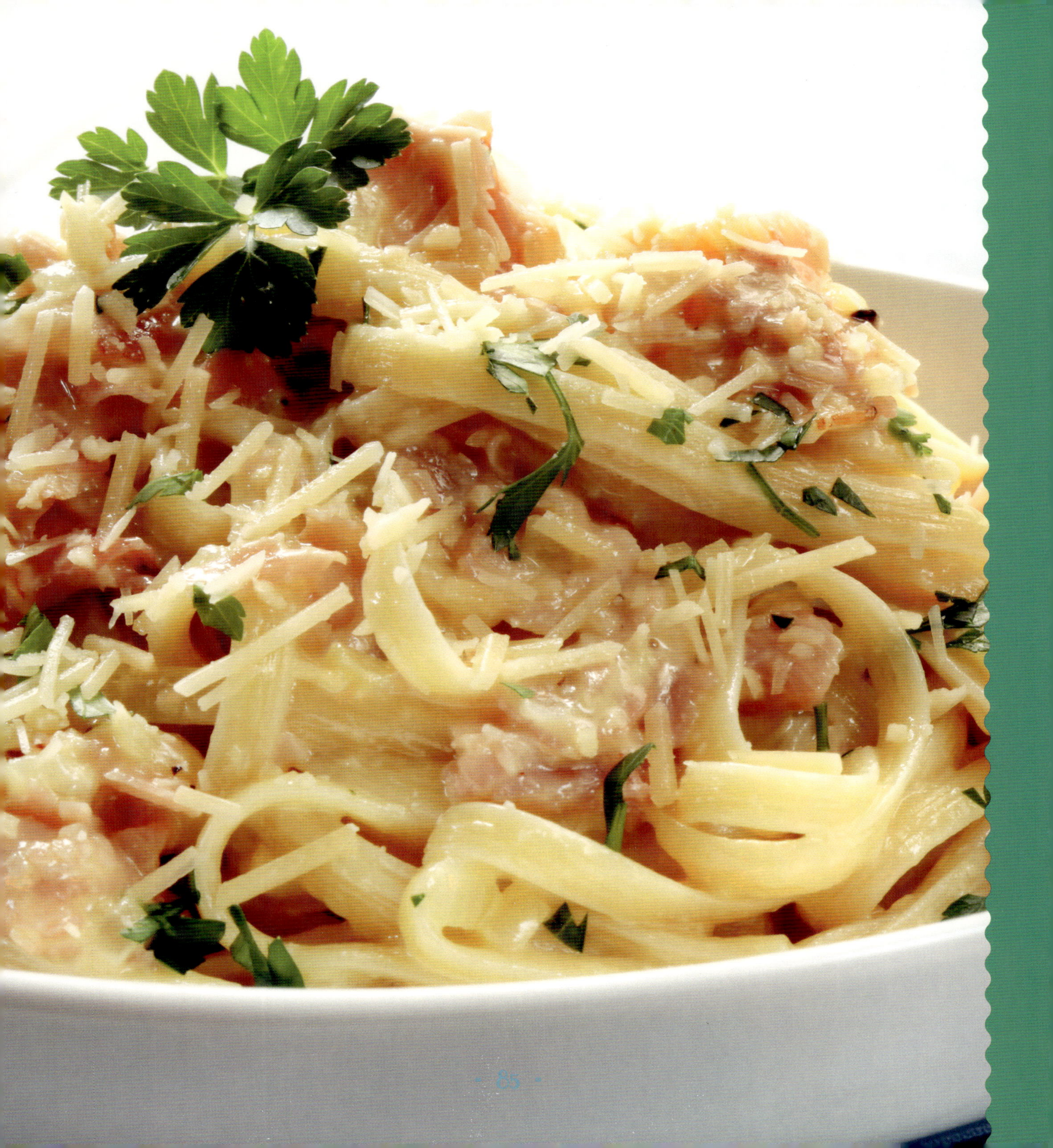

Smoked Bacon and Mushroom Tagliatelle

BY BIAMAITH
WWW.BIAMAITH.IE

2 SERVES — **15 MINUTES** — **20 MINUTES**

INGREDIENTS

160- 200g tagliatelle
6 tbsp Donegal Rapeseed Oil
150– 200g smoked rashers or smoked pancetta
1 garlic clove, chopped
100g mushrooms, finely chopped
¼ fresh red chilli, chopped
3 leaves kale
25g parmesan cheese, then 25g to garnish
Bunch fresh basil or parsley, chopped
3 stalks spring onion or ½ medium onion
Pinch salt and cracked black pepper, to taste

PREPARATION METHOD

Follow the instructions on the pasta packet and cook the desired amount. When the pasta is cooked place it into a colander or sieve and wash it under a cold water tap till cool. This washes the starch from it and stops it from sticking.

Add 2 tbsp Donegal Rapeseed Oil to the pasta and mix well, this will stop it sticking together.

Add the same amount of water back into the empty pot then place it back on to boil.

Heat the Donegal Rapeseed Oil in the pan.

When the pan is hot but not smoking add the pancetta, onion, garlic and chilli, cook for 2 minutes then add the mushrooms and cook for 1 more minute.

Finely chop the kale then add this and cook for 1 minute more.

Gently add the cold cooked pasta back into the pot of hot water from step 4 then stir and leave for about 30 seconds. Strain the water off then add the pasta to the pan with the rest of the ingredients.

Add the chopped herbs and 25g grated parmesan cheese then mix really well.

Taste the dish by tasting a piece of pasta, you may need to add salt and pepper to get that wow flavour you are looking for. I added loads of pepper from a mill and a pinch of salt.

Serve immediately with crusty bread, garlic bread or a nice focaccia.

87

Pork Chops with Sage Tagliatelle

2 SERVES   **10** MINUTES   **30** MINUTES

INGREDIENTS

2 pork loin chops
Sea salt and freshly ground black pepper
100g tagliatelle pasta
100ml cream
6 tbsp Donegal Rapeseed Oil infused with Porcini Mushroom
2 tbsp chopped fresh sage

PREPARATION METHOD

Preheat your oven to 200°C or Gas Mark 6. Season the pork chops on both sides with sea salt and black pepper. Heat 3 tbsp of the Donegal Rapeseed Oil infused with Porcini in a heavy based frying pan until hot.

Sear the pork chops in the hot pan until golden on each side. Remove the chops from the pan and place onto a roasting tray and cook in the oven for 12 minutes or until cooked through.

Cook the pasta as per the instructions on the packet. Meanwhile boil the cream rapidly until reduced and thickened.

Drain the pasta and add to the cream. Add the remaining porcini oil to the pasta, then add the sage. Season with sea salt and black pepper.

Remove pork from the oven and allow to rest for 4-5 minutes. Slice the pork and serve with the pasta.

- 89 -

Pork Belly with Apple Salad and Hickory Smoked Dressing

2 SERVES **20 MINUTES** **10 MINUTES**

INGREDIENTS

2 x 150g portions of slow cooked Irish pork belly, cut into small squares
Sea salt and freshly ground pepper
½ tbsp wholegrain mustard
½ tbsp mayonnaise
6 tbsp Donegal Rapeseed Oil infused with Hickory
1 green apple, cored and finely sliced
80g rocket leaves
25g chopped hazelnuts

PREPARATION METHOD

Reheat the pork belly in a hot oven until piping hot.
Now make the dressing. Place the wholegrain mustard and mayonnaise into a bowl.

Whisk together until smooth. Slowly whisk in the Donegal Rapeseed Oil infused with Hickory a tablespoon at a time to form a dressing. If the dressing is a little thick, add a teaspoon of boiling water to thin slightly. Season with sea salt and black pepper.

Place the sliced apple and rocket into a bowl and dress with some of the dressing.

Serve the pork belly on a plate, place the salad in the middle of the plate and sprinkle with the chopped hazelnuts.

Drizzle the remaining dressing around the plate.

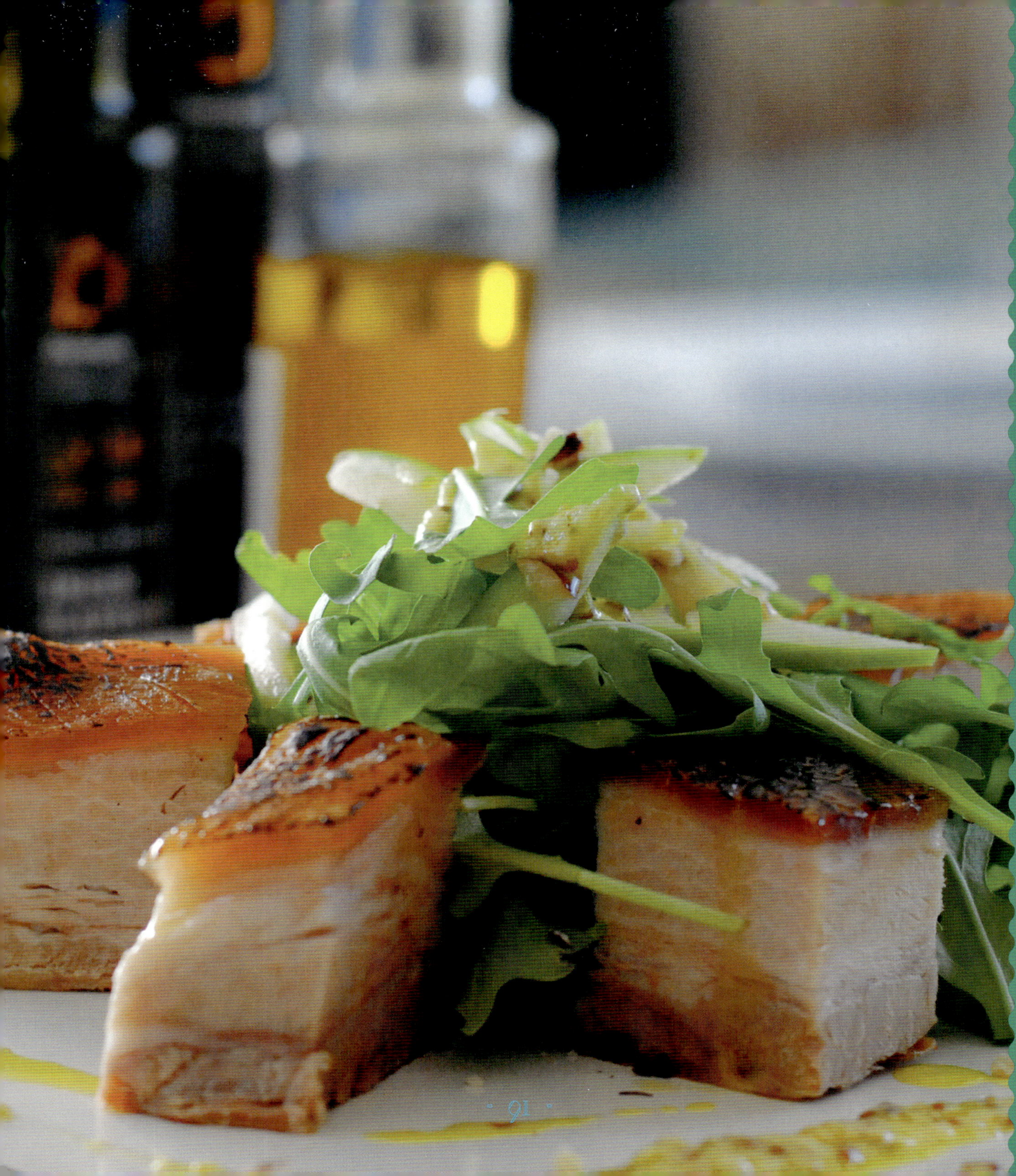

Chorizo and Salami Pizza

8 SERVES **25** MINUTES **20** MINUTES

INGREDIENTS

Pizza Dough

(Makes 2 large bases)

1 tbsp Donegal Rapeseed Oil

320g strong white flour

½ tsp salt

1 tsp sugar

Half a 7g sachet fast action dried yeast

150ml warm water

Toppings

½ cup pizza sauce

1 cup mozzarella cheese, grated

100g ham, chopped

8 slices of salami, halved

1 chorizo sausage, thinly sliced

½ red onion, thinly sliced, optional

½ green pepper, sliced, optional

Handful of mushrooms, sliced, optional

PREPARATION METHOD

Preheat the oven to 230°C.

Using a food mixer, mix together the flour, salt, sugar and yeast at slow speed. Add the Donegal Rapeseed Oil and water and mix for 5 minutes on a higher speed to create a soft dough.

Leave in a warm place until doubled in size. Remove from the bowl and knead gently to the original size. Cut the dough in half and shape each piece into a ball. Using a rolling pin on a lightly floured surface, roll the dough out into a large thin round shape.

Spread the dough evenly with pizza sauce and sprinkle with half the cheese. Top with ham, salami, chorizo, onion, peppers and mushrooms. Sprinkle with the remaining cheese.

Place the pizza on a round baking tray. Bake for 15 to 20 minutes or until base is golden and crispy and the cheese is melted.

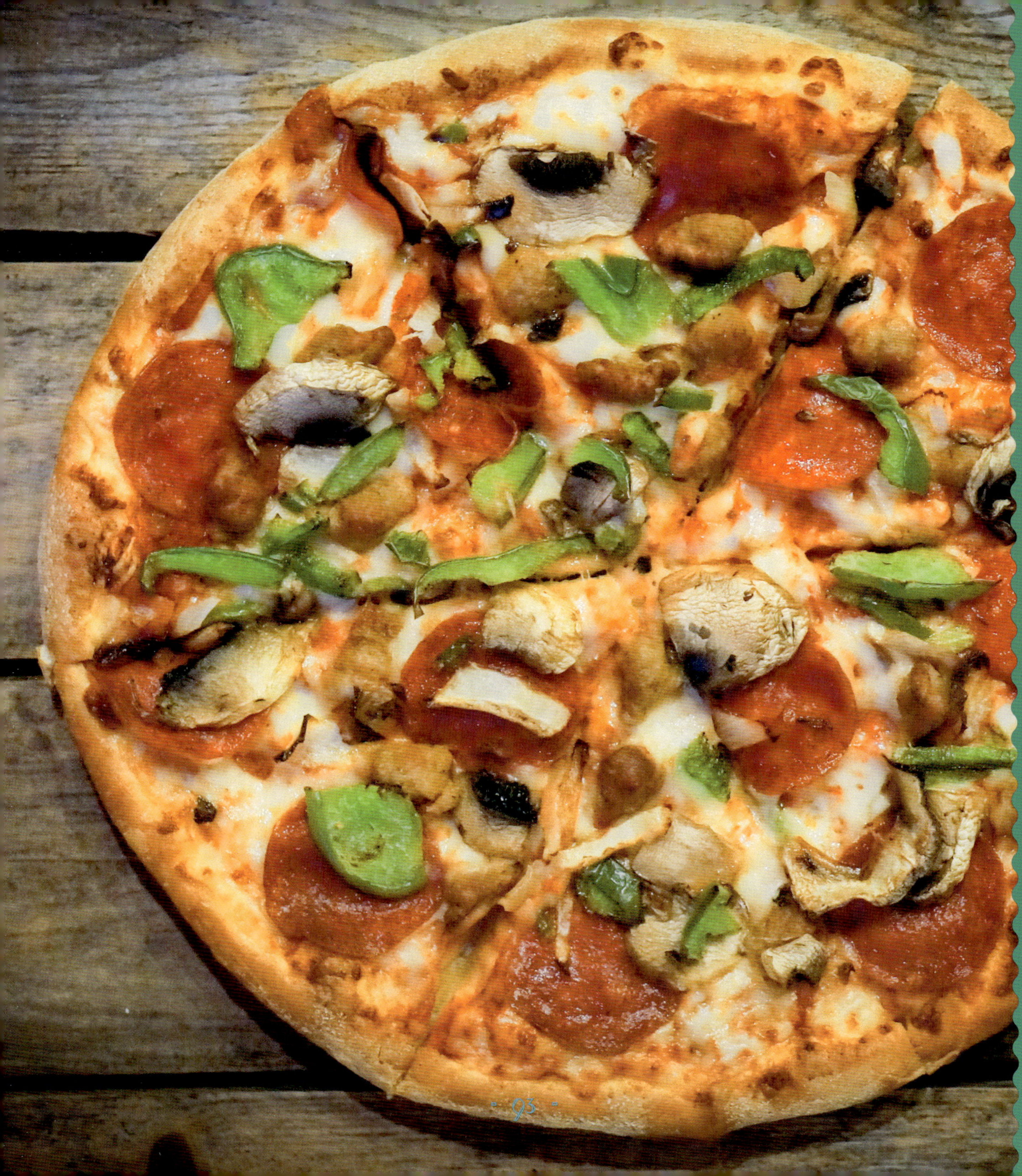

Chilli Beef Burger with Chilli Jam

BY THE IRISH FOOD GUIDE
WWW.IRISHFOODGUIDE.IE

4 SERVES   **15 MINUTES**   **20 MINUTES**

INGREDIENTS

500g lean minced beef
100g finely diced onion
2 tbsp Donegal Rapeseed Oil infused with Chilli
1 red chilli chopped finely
Ground black pepper and salt
2 ripe tomatoes finely chopped
2 tbsp sugar
4 brioche baps
Rocket salad for garnish

PREPARATION METHOD

Mix together the minced beef with 1 tbsp Donegal Rapeseed Oil infused with Chilli, half of the finely diced onion and half of the chopped red chilli. Season with ground black pepper and salt.

Shape into 4 even-sized burgers and leave aside for ten minutes for the flavours to merge with the meat.

Meanwhile, combine the chopped tomato, the rest of the onion, the rest of the chilli, the sugar and the other 1 tbsp Donegal Rapeseed Oil infused with Chilli in a small pot.

Bring this gently to the boil and then turn the heat down to low and cook out until all the liquid is evaporated and the jam has thickened.

Spoon the chilli jam into a small jar and place in the fridge to cool.

Heat your frying pan to very hot and place the burgers on the dry pan. Leave them untouched for 30 seconds to sear the outside of the meat and then turn them over.

Turn the heat down to half and let the burgers cook out.

Cut your baps in half and warm them under the grill or in the oven.

When the meat is cooked through, build up your burgers with the rocket salad and a little mayonnaise on the buns and the beef burger topped with chilli jam.

Serve immediately.

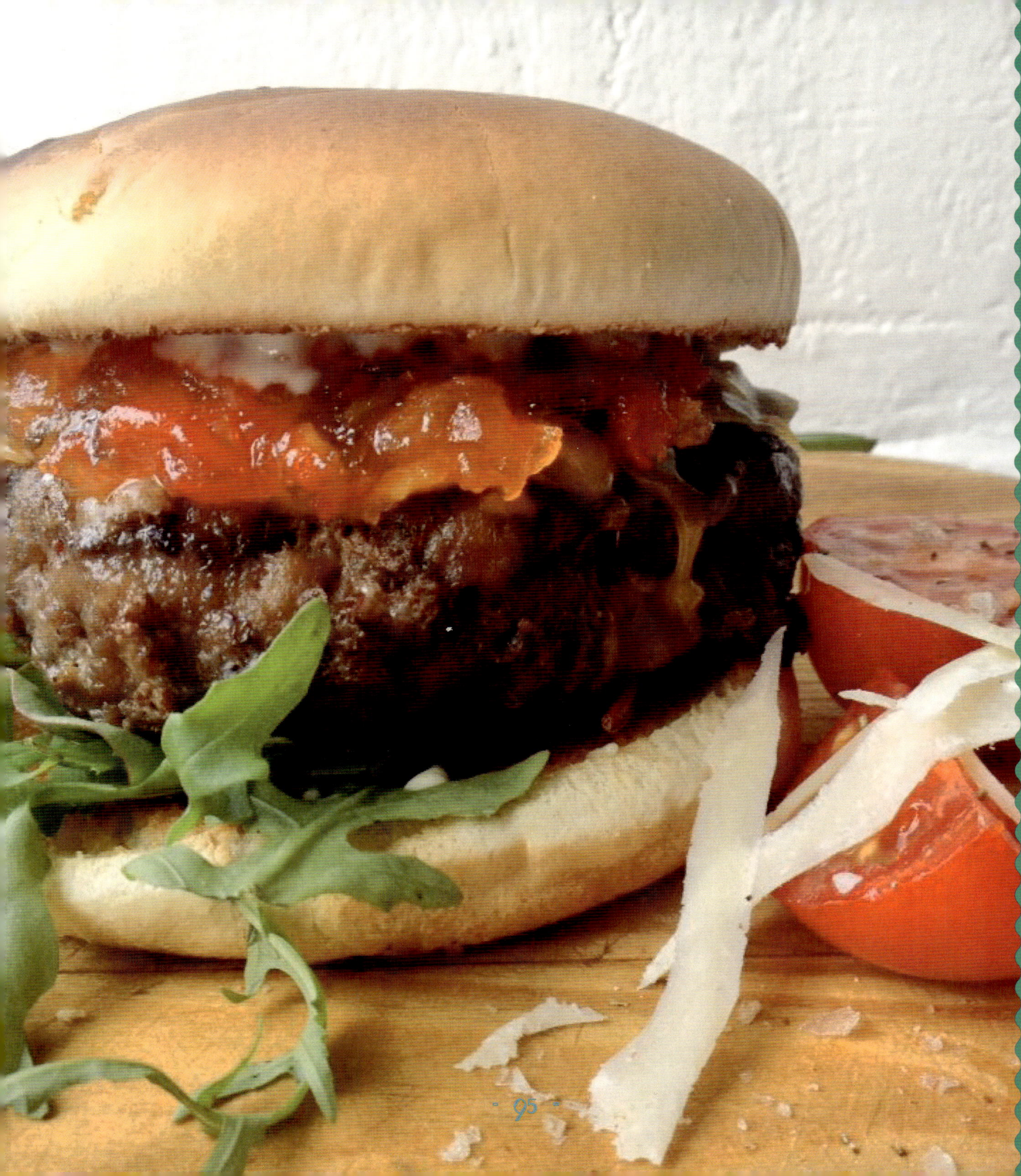

Chilli Con Carne

4 SERVES   **50** MINUTES   **70** MINUTES

INGREDIENTS

- 1 tbsp Donegal Rapeseed Oil
- 1 onion, chopped
- 1 red pepper, chopped
- 2 garlic cloves, peeled
- 1 heaped tsp chilli powder
- 1 tsp paprika
- 1 tsp ground cumin
- 500g lean minced beef
- 1 beef stock cube
- 400g tin chopped tomatoes
- ½ tsp dried marjoram
- 1 tsp sugar, optional
- 2 tbsp tomato purée
- 410g tin red kidney beans
- Plain long grain rice, to serve
- Sour cream, to serve

PREPARATION METHOD

Finely chop a large onion. Cut 1 red pepper in half lengthways, remove stalk and wash the seeds away, then chop. Peel and finely chop 2 garlic cloves.

Put your pan on the hob over a medium heat. Add the Donegal Rapeseed Oil and leave it for 1-2 minutes until hot. Add the onions and cook, stirring frequently, for about 5 minutes, or until the onions are soft and slightly translucent. Add the garlic, red pepper, 1 heaped tsp chilli powder, 1 tsp paprika and 1 tsp ground cumin. Stir well, then leave it to cook for another 5 minutes, stirring occasionally.

Brown the 500g lean minced beef. Turn the heat up a bit, add the meat to the pan and break it up with your spoon. Keep stirring for at least 5 minutes, until all the mince is broken up and there are no more pink bits. Make sure you keep the heat hot enough for the meat to fry and become brown, rather than just stew.

Crumble 1 beef stock cube into 300ml hot water. Pour this into the pan with the mince mixture. Open 1 can of chopped tomatoes and add these to the mix. Add in ½ tsp dried marjoram and 1 tsp sugar, if using, and add a good pinch of salt and pepper. Add about 2 tbsp tomato purée and stir the sauce well.

Simmer it gently. Bring to the boil, give it a good stir and put a lid on the pan. Turn down the heat until it is gently bubbling and leave it for 20 minutes. You should check on the pan occasionally to stir it and make sure the sauce doesn't catch on the bottom of the pan or isn't drying out. If it is, add a couple of tablespoons of water and make sure that the heat is low enough.

Drain and rinse 1 can of red kidney beans in a sieve and stir them into the chilli pot. Bring to the boil again, and gently bubble without the lid for another 10 minutes, adding a little more water if it looks too dry. Taste a bit of the chilli and season. Now replace the lid, turn off the heat and leave your chilli to stand for 10 minutes before serving.

Serve with sour cream and boiled rice.

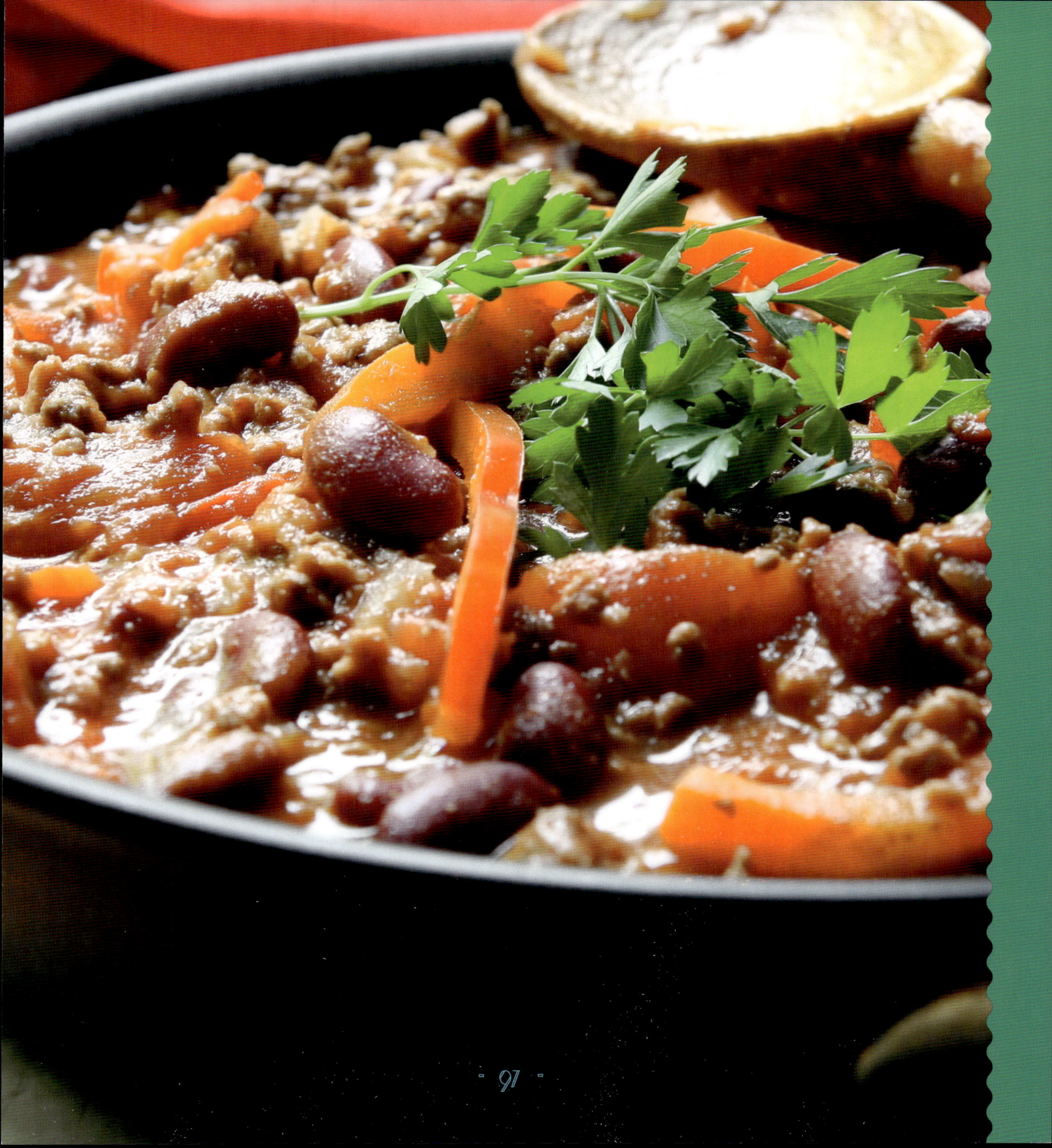

Fillet of Beef with Chunky Chips and Mushrooms

4 SERVES **15 MINUTES** **60 MINUTES**

INGREDIENTS

4 fillet steaks, about 200g each

Mushrooms

500ml Donegal Rapeseed Oil

4 garlic cloves, crushed

1 rosemary leaf, finely chopped

1 thyme leaf, finely chopped

4 flat cap mushrooms, stems removed and caps peeled

Chunky Chips

1kg potatoes, peeled

Salt and pepper

5 garlic cloves, unpeeled

Thyme and rosemary sprigs

Donegal Rapeseed Oil

PREPARATION METHOD

Preheat oven to 130°C.

Prepare the mushrooms. Mix together the Donegal Rapeseed Oil, garlic, rosemary and thyme. Put the mushrooms gill-side up on a non-stick baking tray, pour over the oil mixture and season well with salt and pepper. Roast for one hour.

For the chunky chips, cut the potatoes in thick chips. Parboil in a pan of salted water for 5-10 minutes until just tender when pricked with a skewer. Drain and pat dry with a tea towel. Place onto a roasting tray and scatter over the garlic and herbs. Generously drizzle with the Donegal Rapeseed Oil and sprinkle with salt and pepper. Toss them to coat them in the oil and flavourings. Cook in the oven for 10-15 minutes turning them a few times until the chips are golden brown and crisp. Drain on kitchen paper and serve immediately.

Heat a heavy frying pan until red hot and add a little Donegal Rapeseed Oil. Season the steaks all over. Place the steaks in the pan and seal the top, bottom and sides then transfer to a hot tray and finish in the oven. Allow 5 minutes for medium to rare meat and work up from there.

To serve, put some mushrooms in the middle of the plate and place the steak on top. Serve immediately with the chunky chips.

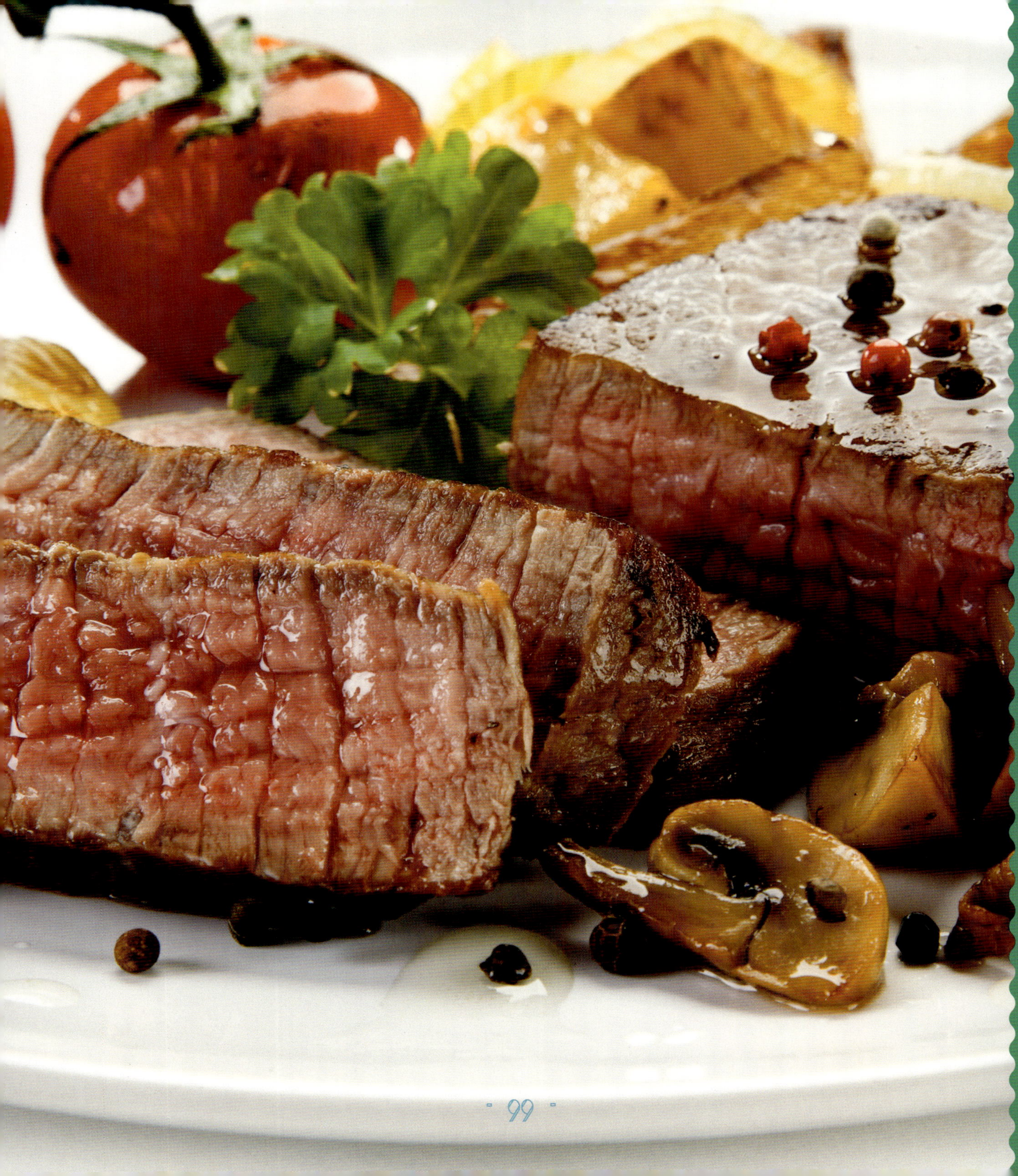

Beef Fajitas

BY I LOVE COOKING
WWW.ILOVECOOKING.IE

4-6 SERVES | **5 MINUTES** | **10 MINUTES**

INGREDIENTS

400-500g minute steaks, cut into thin strips
2 tsp ground cumin
2 tsp ground coriander
½ tsp smoked paprika
Sea salt flakes
Donegal Rapeseed Oil, for cooking
1 red onion, sliced
1 red bell pepper, sliced
1 yellow bell pepper, sliced

To Serve
8 tortilla wraps
Fresh coriander, roughly chopped
Grated cheese
Salsa
Sour Cream

PREPARATION METHOD

Toss the beef with the spices and large pinch of salt.

Heat a large pan on medium high heat with a dash of Donegal Rapeseed Oil. Once hot, add the seasoned beef and cook for 2-3 minutes.
Lower the heat to medium and add the onion and bell peppers and another pinch of salt. Cook, tossing occasionally, until vegetables have softened but still have a bit of a bite.

Remove from the pan, strew with chopped coriander then serve with warmed tortilla wraps and other fajita favourites like Manchego cheese, salsa and sour cream.

- 101 -

Beef Lasagne

BY BIA MAITH
WWW.BIAMAITH.IE

6-8 SERVES | **30 MINUTES** | **25 MINUTES**

INGREDIENTS

450g steak mince

1 x 400g tin of chopped tomatoes

500g of tomato passata

4 garlic cloves, chopped

1 medium onion

1 tbsp dried oregano

1-2 large carrots

1 bell pepper

4 smoked rashers, chopped

1-2 kale leaves

1 beef stock cube

¼ tsp black pepper

2 tbsp Donegal Rapeseed Oil

100g grated cheddar cheese

12 cherry tomatoes

Cheese Sauce

400ml milk

20g butter or margarine

20g plain flour

100g cheddar cheese grated

1 vegetable stock cube

PREPARATION METHOD

Chop the onion, pepper, garlic, carrots and kale into really small pieces, set to one side.

Heat the Donegal Rapeseed Oil in the pan then fry the mince and rashers. Break it up so it is free from lumps.

When the mince is brown add the chopped vegetables and cook for 2-3 minutes.

Add the tin of chopped tomatoes, passata, oregano and stock cube. Stir well then turn the heat right down and simmer for 15 minutes.

Preheat your oven to 180°C or Gas Mark 4. In the meantime, melt the butter in the microwave then add the flour and mix really well so they are combined to make a roux.

Heat the milk in the pot until it is almost boiling then add the cheese and the stock cube and stir well for about 1 minute.

Add half the roux and whisk until it is combined, it will thicken the sauce. If it isn't thick enough, add more.

Remove both the meat sauce and cheese sauce from the heat and get a dish for your lasagne.

Spread a layer of the meat sauce on the bottom of the dish.

Add a layer of the lasagne sheets. Try not to overlap them as they may not cook through and don't be afraid to break a few sheets to make them fit.

Keep doing this until you have used all the mince and are left with a layer of lasagne sheets on top.

Pour the cheese sauce on top with the rest of the cheese. Place the cherry tomatoes on top.

Place onto a baking tray to catch any drips and bake for 20-25 minutes.

Remove from the oven and either serve immediately or allow to cool if you plan on freezing it.

Once cool it is really easy to cut and portion. Wrap each portion in cling film then freeze for up to 1 month.

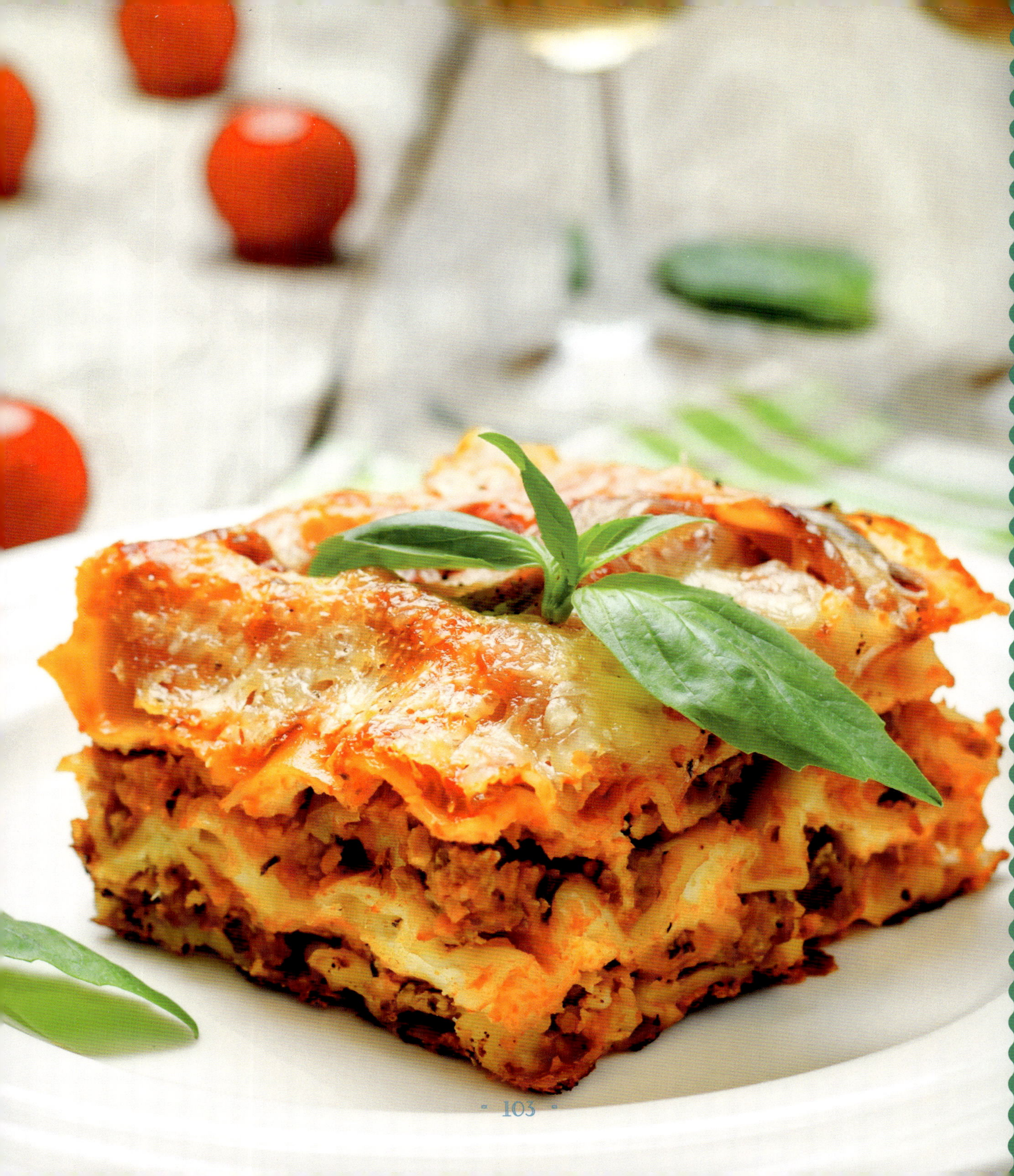

The Perfect Steak

BY CHEF BRIAN MCDERMOTT

WWW.CHEFBRIANMCDERMOTT.COM

4 SERVES   **10 MINUTES**   **20 MINUTES**

INGREDIENTS

- 4 steaks sirloin, rump or rib eye
- 40ml brandy
- ½ chopped onion
- 4 mushrooms
- 150ml crème fraiche or cream
- Drop of Worchester sauce
- 12 green peppercorns or cracked black pepper
- 1 clove garlic chopped
- Freshly ground pepper to season
- 100ml beef stock
- Drizzle of Donegal Rapeseed Oil

PREPARATION METHOD

Allow steak to sit at room temperature.

Preheat a frying pan and drizzle with Donegal Rapeseed Oil and place steaks in the pan. Do not agitate steaks. Leave for approximately 3 minutes then turn.

Season with ground black pepper. Cook for a further 2 minutes.

Transfer the steaks to a hot tray and finish in the oven if required for medium - well done. If you require medium – rare, just let the steak rest.

In the same pan as steak was in, add chopped onion, garlic and mushrooms followed by peppercorns.

Cook for few minutes then add the brandy and flambé.

Straight away, add beef stock and crème fraiche or cream. Reduce heat and allow to reduce until sauce thickens. Add a drop of Worchester sauce.

Serve sauce beside steak not over it.

BRIAN WAS BORN AND RAISED IN BURT, CO. DONEGAL. AS ONE OF TWELVE CHILDREN, THE FOCAL POINT OF THE FAMILY WAS ALWAYS HIS MOTHER'S KITCHEN TABLE, AND HER HOME COOKING CONTINUES TO INSPIRE BRIAN AS HE SHARES HIS OWN LOVE OF FOOD WITH OTHERS.

BRIAN IS ONE OF FEW IRISH CHEFS TO HOLD A CULINARY ARTS DEGREE, GRADUATING TOP OF HIS CLASS, AND HE WENT ON TO HAVE A SUCCESSFUL CAREER AS A CHEF IN SOME OF DONEGAL'S TOP KITCHENS. HE WAS A SENIOR GLOBAL PRODUCT DEVELOPER FOR KERRY GROUP WHEN, AGED 32, HE WAS DIAGNOSED WITH A HEART CONDITION.

FORCED TO RE-EVALUATE HIS PRIORITIES, BRIAN BECAME A CHAMPION FOR HEALTHY FOOD WHICH WAS TASTY AND AFFORDABLE, AND, FUELLED BY A DESIRE TO PASS THAT KNOWLEDGE ON TO OTHERS, BEGAN TEACHING SCHOOLS AND COMMUNITY GROUPS IN HIS LOCAL AREA.

TODAY HE IS A POPULAR CELEBRITY CHEF WHO IS A REGULAR BOTH ON THE IRISH FOOD FESTIVAL CIRCUIT AND ON RTE AND BBC TELEVISION AND RADIO. HE RUNS HIS OWN COOKERY SCHOOL IN MOVILLE, CO. DONEGAL, IS A FOOD CONSULTANT FOR MAJOR IRISH COMPANIES, AND IS GENERAL MANAGER OF THE FOODOVATION FOOD DEVELOPMENT CENTRE IN THE NORTH WEST REGIONAL COLLEGE IN DERRY.

HE IS ALSO THE AUTHOR OF THE SUCCESSFUL COOKERY BOOK, 'REUNITE WITH FOOD', AND IS LOOKING FORWARD TO PUBLISHING HIS SECOND BOOK LATER THIS YEAR.

Fillet Steak with Potato Millefeuille, Roasted Cherry Tomatoes, White Truffle Butter and Crispy Onion Rings

BY CHEF GER LYNCH

6 SERVES **50 MINUTES** **55 MINUTES**

INGREDIENTS

6 beef fillet steaks, approx. 6-8oz
Drizzle Donegal Rapeseed Oil

Millefeuille Potatoes
6 large rooster potatoes
500g salted butter
Pinch salt or white pepper

Roasted Cherry Tomatoes
1 punnet cherry tomatoes
5ml Donegal Rapeseed Oil infused with Fennel
1 garlic clove
Pinch black pepper
Few sprigs thyme

PREPARATION METHOD

It's best to do your millefeuille potato the evening before. This beautiful potato dish needs time to rest and you can also get the perfect cut when it's cold. Preheat the oven to 180°C.

Melt butter in the microwave. Peel potatoes and cut length ways as thin as possible, add to the melted butter and add a little salt and pepper.

Line a small square deep dish with greaseproof paper and layer the potatoes right to the top, place another sheet of grease proof paper on top and press firmly all over and make sure it's even.

Cover with tin foil and bake in oven for 55 minutes at 180°C.

When cooked, you need to press the dish with something a similar size; I use the same dish as it fits perfectly. Leave to cool down slowly and press overnight in your fridge. The following day run a small knife across the edges to loosen the potato, flip onto a chopping board and cut into the appropriate size. Place on a baking tray lined with greaseproof paper ready for reheating.

You can also make your white truffle butter the evening before. Make sure the butter is at room temperature, dice and place in a large bowl.

Peel and dice the shallot as finely as possible. Sweat in a pan without colour on a low heat with a small bit of the butter. When soft, add shallots to the butter, finely chop the parsley and add to the butter, add the Donegal Rapeseed Oil infused with White Truffle and cracked black pepper, mix well.

White Truffle Butter

250g salted butter

5ml Donegal Rapeseed Oil infused with White Truffle

1 large shallot

1 small packet parsley

Pinch cracked black pepper

Crispy Onion Rings

2 large onions

400g self-raising flour

500ml sparkling water

Pinch salt or white pepper

Lay a large amount of cling film on your table and place butter on top. Start to roll into a small cylinder shape (it may be easier to do in small amounts), twist edges and seal. Leave in fridge over night to set. You can cut the butter into thin slices, place evenly and store in a cool place until serving time.

Preheat deep fat fryer to 180°C for the onion rings. Cut onions into thin rings, dip into flour and leave to the side. In a large bowl mix the flour, sparkling water, salt and pepper with a whisk to form the batter. Dip the floured rings into the batter letting all the excess drip back into the bowl and add straight to the fryer slowly. It's best to do 3 or 4 at a time, you can keep warm in the oven if needed. You should have the millefeuille potato back in the oven now to heat, cook for 20 to 25 minutes.

On a separate tray, add half the cherry tomatoes, add the thyme, chopped garlic, cracked black pepper and Donegal Rapeseed Oil infused with Fennel. Toss all ingredients well and finish in the oven for 6 minutes.

Season the fillet steaks with salt and pepper on both sides, heat a large frying pan with a little Donegal Rapeseed Oil, seal the steaks in the pan on both sides getting an all over dark golden colour.

I like my steak medium rare, this will take 6 to 8 minutes in the pan, depending on your preference. If you like it a little more cooked you can finish cooking in the oven; medium should take 12 to 14 minutes and well done 18 to 20 minutes.

After cooking, leave the steaks to rest for a few mins on a wire rack. Place the butter on top of all the steaks so it melts a little but not too much. At this stage all other ingredients should be piping hot and ready to serve.

Irish Ribeye with Fresh Tomato Salsa and Smoky Paprika Potatoes

BY DROP CHEF
WWW.DROPCHEF.COM

2 SERVES | **10 MINUTES** | **30 MINUTES**

INGREDIENTS

280g baby potatoes
12 cherry tomatoes
1 red onion
2 spring onions
5g fresh parsley
5g fresh tarragon
1 garlic clove
1 red chilli
2 x 180g ribeye steaks
5g smoked paprika
Salt and pepper
4 tbsp Donegal Rapeseed Oil

PREPARATION METHOD

Cook the potatoes in a pot of boiling salted water until tender. When the potatoes are cooked, strain them and set aside.

Cut the tomatoes into quarters. Remove the outer layer from the red onion and finely chop. Slice the spring onion. Chop the tarragon and parsley. Finely chop the garlic. Remove the seeds from the chilli and finely dice it. Set all the ingredients aside.

In a bowl, combine the tomatoes, garlic, chopped onion, herbs, spring onion and 4 tablespoons of Donegal Rapeseed Oil. Add the chopped chilli to taste. Season with salt and pepper.

When the potatoes are cooked, slice them and set aside.

Put a pan on a high heat and fry the steak in a drop of Donegal Rapeseed Oil for 1-2 minutes. Remove the steak from the pan and cover with foil to keep warm.

Using the same pan fry the potatoes in a little Donegal Rapeseed Oil for 3 minutes. Add the smoked paprika and cook for another minute.

Serve the steak with the paprika potatoes and spoon over the fresh salsa.

PHOTO CREDIT: COLIN JUDGE

White Chocolate Tart with Strawberry Lavender Compote

BY NEIL FERGUSON OF CASTLEMARTYR RESORT

8 SERVES | **60 MINUTES** | **30 MINUTES**

INGREDIENTS

PASTRY
550g Flour
¼ tsp salt
95ml Donegal Rapeseed Oil
90ml soy milk
15g sugar
30ml Donegal Rapeseed Oil infused with Fennel

WHITE CHOCOLATE GANACHE
300g White Chocolate
150ml cream
25g caster sugar
38g Donegal Rapeseed Oil

STRAWBERRY LAVENDER COMPOTE
300g strawberries
100g caster sugar
½ tsp lavender
50ml water

PREPARATION METHOD

Add everything except the egg and mix until a sandy texture.

Add the egg. Mix until combined.

Rest for 1 hour. Roll out and line tart mould.

Rest for another half hour. Blind bake tart base for 15 mins at 180°C.

Remove blind bake. Brush with egg yolk and bake for a further 5 mins.

Cool to get ready for ganache.

Heat the cream and sugar.

Pour over chocolate.

Once melted drizzle in Donegal Rapeseed Oil to create an emulsion.

Pour into the tart straight away to get a smooth top.

Add water, sugar and lavender to a pan and bring to the boil.

Infuse for 20 minutes. Strain into another pot, discard lavender.

Wash and dry strawberries. Chop the strawberries and add to the syrup.

Bring to the boil. Remove from heat and cool.

Serve.

NEIL FERGUSON HAS OVER 15 YEARS OF EXPERIENCE WORKING IN KITCHENS THROUGHOUT THE UK, AUSTRALIA AND IRELAND.
DURING HIS STUDIES NEIL BEGAN WORKING IN THE KILLARNEY PARK HOTEL WHERE HE WORKED HIS WAY UP TO SOUS CHEF. NEIL WORKED UNDER THE TUTELAGE OF ODRAN LUCY, WHOSE CLASSICAL TRAINING IN MICHELIN STAR RESTAURANTS HELPED TO HONE HIS SKILLS AS A CHEF AND KITCHEN MANAGER.
LOOKING TO START A NEW CHAPTER IN HIS CAREER NEIL, ALONG WITH HIS WIFE AND DAUGHTER, MADE THE MOVE TO CASTLEMARTYR TO TAKE UP HIS CURRENT POSITION AS HEAD PASTRY CHEF AT THE CASTLEMARTYR RESORT.
A TRUE CREATIVE, NEIL'S ELEGANT AND IMAGINATIVE DESSERTS ARE ALWAYS A HIGHLIGHT FOR THE GUESTS. WHEN HE'S NOT IN THE KITCHEN, NEIL ENJOYS SHARING HIS CREATIVE DESSERTS WITH HIS SOCIAL MEDIA FOLLOWERS.

Elderflower Jelly, Fresh Fruit and Sorbet

BY MULBERRY GARDEN
WWW.MULBERRYGARDEN.IE

6 SERVES **20 MINUTES** **-**

INGREDIENTS

16g powdered gelatin

35g glucose

150ml water

190g white sugar

150g Donegal Rapeseed Oil

10g elderflower cordial

Fresh fruit and sorbet or ice cream, to serve

PREPARATION METHOD

Bloom gelatin by placing a small amount of cold water in a shallow bowl. Sprinkle the gelatin evenly over the top of the water. It will begin to absorb the water and swell in size. Let the mixture stand for 5 minutes before proceeding with the recipe. You will need about ¼ cup of water per 7g of gelatin.

Heat water, sugar and glucose to 95°C, stirring constantly. Take off the heat.

Blend in the Donegal Rapeseed Oil, add the gelatin and 10g of elderflower cordial.

Let the mixture infuse for 10 minutes, then strain into the mould or plastic tray.

Keep it in the fridge before use.

Serve with sorbet or ice cream and fresh seasonal fruits.

MULBERRY GARDEN IS HIDDEN DOWN MULBERRY LANE IN DONNYBROOK. IT IS SITUATED IN THE GROUNDS OF AN OLD COTTAGE DATING FROM 1911. WE OPENED OUR DOORS AS MULBERRY GARDEN IN 2011. HERE IN MULBERRY GARDEN WE ARE VERY PROUD OF OUR LITTLE ISLAND AND ARE PASSIONATE ABOUT USING ALL THINGS IRISH. FROM THE MOMENT YOU WALK THROUGH THE DOOR YOU ARE SURROUNDED BY IRELAND. OUR WALLS ARE ADORNED WITH IRISH WOOL, PAINTINGS BY IRISH ARTISTS AND QUOTES FROM THE GREAT OSCAR WILDE. OUR TABLES ARE DRESSED IN IRISH LINEN, NEWBRIDGE SILVER CUTLERY, NATIVE WOODEN BREAD BOARDS, IRISH ATLANTIC SEA SALT AND DONEGAL RAPESEED OIL.

SO, OF COURSE, OUR HEAD CHEF IS FERVENT ABOUT USING IRISH INGREDIENTS. EVERY WEEK HE BRINGS YOU A DIFFERENT MENU USING ONLY INGREDIENTS THAT ARE IN SEASON. HE WORKS WITH THE BEST LOCAL FARMERS, BUTCHERS, FISHERMEN AND ARTISAN PRODUCERS TO BRING YOU AN EXCITING AND UNIQUE MENU WHICH CELEBRATES THE DELICIOUS AND WONDERFUL FOOD HERITAGE OF IRELAND.

Perfect Scones

8-10 SERVES | **15 MINUTES** | **20 MINUTES**

INGREDIENTS

2 cups plain flour
3½ tsp baking powder
½ tsp salt
¼ cup Donegal Rapeseed Oil
⅔ cup of milk
1 egg
Butter, jam and cream, to serve

PREPARATION METHOD

Preheat the oven to 180°C. Lightly grease a large baking tray.

Sift together the flour, baking powder and salt. Beat the egg together with the milk and Donegal Rapeseed Oil. Make a well in the centre of the flour and pour the liquid into it. Then mix using a wooden spoon.

Mix until all the liquid has been absorbed but do not overmix. If there is still some dry flour visible, add milk a tablespoon at a time and mix until all the flour is absorbed. The mixture should be sticky but firm enough to hold its shape.

Press the dough out on a flat clean floured surface until it is about 5mm thick. Cut out your scones using a floured round cutter and place them on a baking tray.

Bake for 15 to 20 minutes or until golden – test with a toothpick to see if they are done.
Serve still warm with butter, jam and cream.

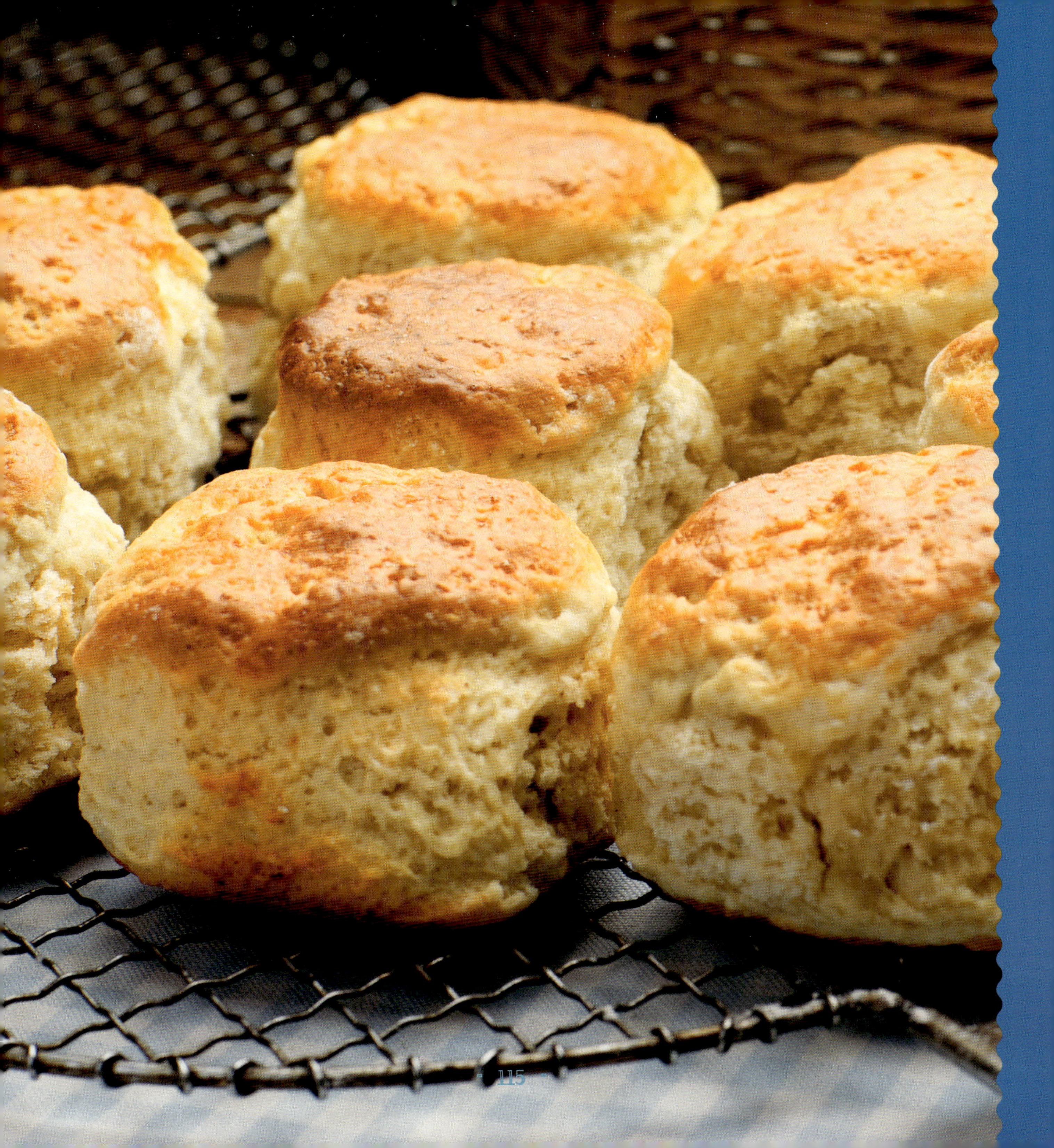

Irish Soda Bread

12 SERVES   **10 MINUTES**   **40 MINUTES**

INGREDIENTS

500g plain flour

4 tbsp caster sugar

1 tsp bicarbonate of soda

2 tsp baking powder

1 tsp salt

2 eggs

275g buttermilk

4 tbsp Donegal Rapeseed Oil

175g raisins, optional

PREPARATION METHOD

Preheat oven to 180°C or Gas Mark 4. Grease a baking tray or line with parchment.
In a large bowl, stir together the flour, sugar, bicarbonate of soda, baking powder and salt.

In another bowl, whisk together the eggs, buttermilk and Donegal Rapeseed Oil. Make a well in the centre of the flour mixture and pour in the buttermilk mixture.

Add the raisins and stir a few times, just until the ingredients come together into a soft dough. Turn the dough out onto a floured surface and with floured hands shape dough into a ball. Place the dough on the prepared baking tray and cut a large cross in the top with a sharp knife.

Place the bread on a middle rack of the preheated oven, and bake until golden brown, 30 to 40 minutes.

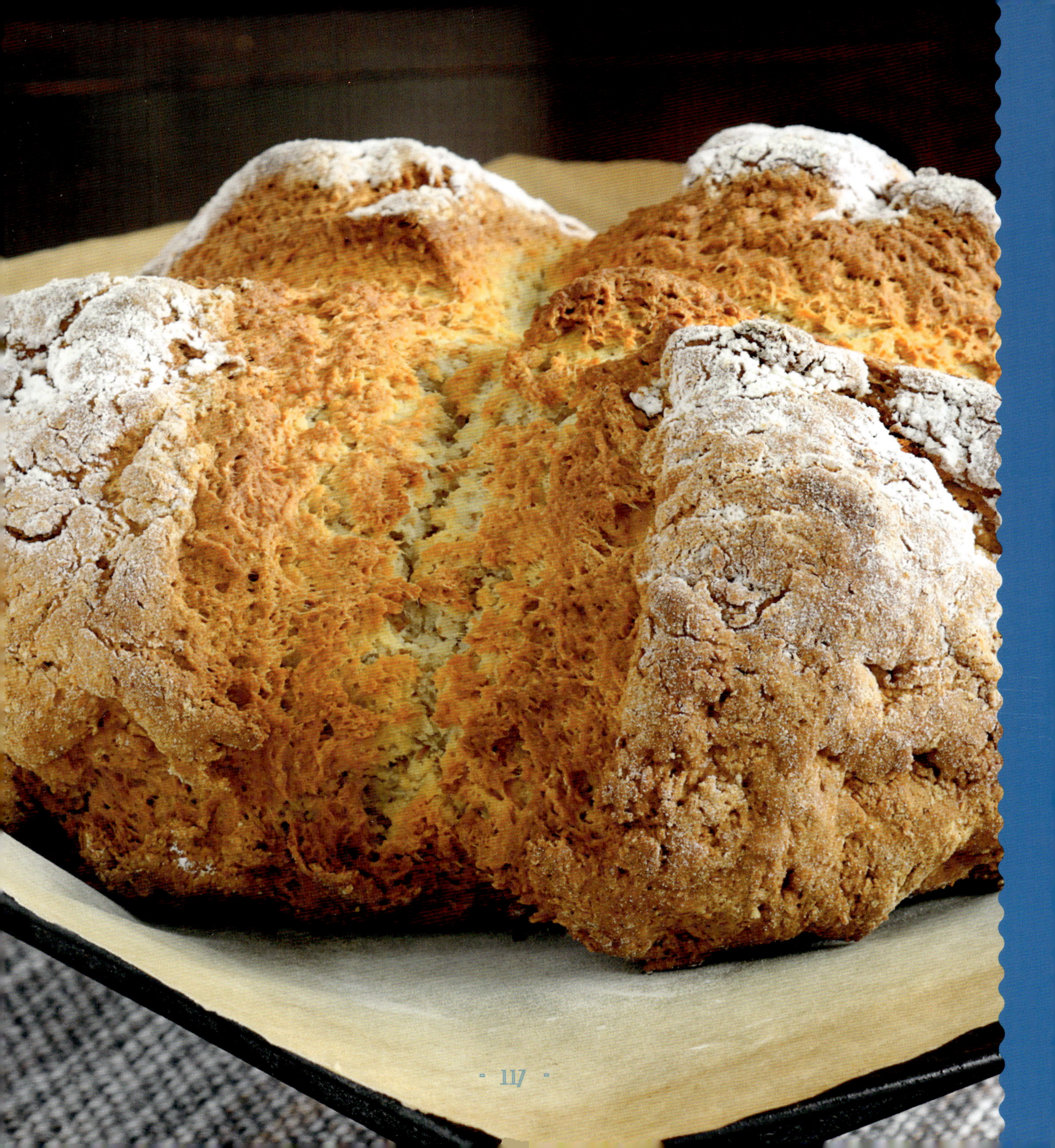

Cheese and Onion Yeast Bread

3 LOAVES | 60 MINUTES | 20 MINUTES

INGREDIENTS

650g strong flour
7g instant yeast
85g Donegal Rapeseed Oil
450g warm water
50g cheddar cheese
½ onion, diced

PREPARATION METHOD

Sieve the flour and yeast and mix together in a bowl. Make a well in the centre of the flour mix and add the Donegal Rapeseed Oil plus warm water and mix dough until all ingredients are evenly distributed.
The dough should be smooth but a little sticky.

Flour the table really well and stretch dough to double the length in a clockwise turn. Return dough to the bowl and cover with cling film and allow the dough to ferment and double in size for 45-60 minutes in a warm part of the kitchen.

Fry ½ diced onion and add to dough with 50g grated cheese. Then turn out to the table again and knead until you have a smooth non-sticky dough, add more flour if required.
Split dough into three and flavour each to your choice. Shape and add to 1lb loaf tin and allow dough to double once more.

Bake in a preheated oven at 200°C for 20 minutes.
Wrap bread in a clean dry tea towel to cool.

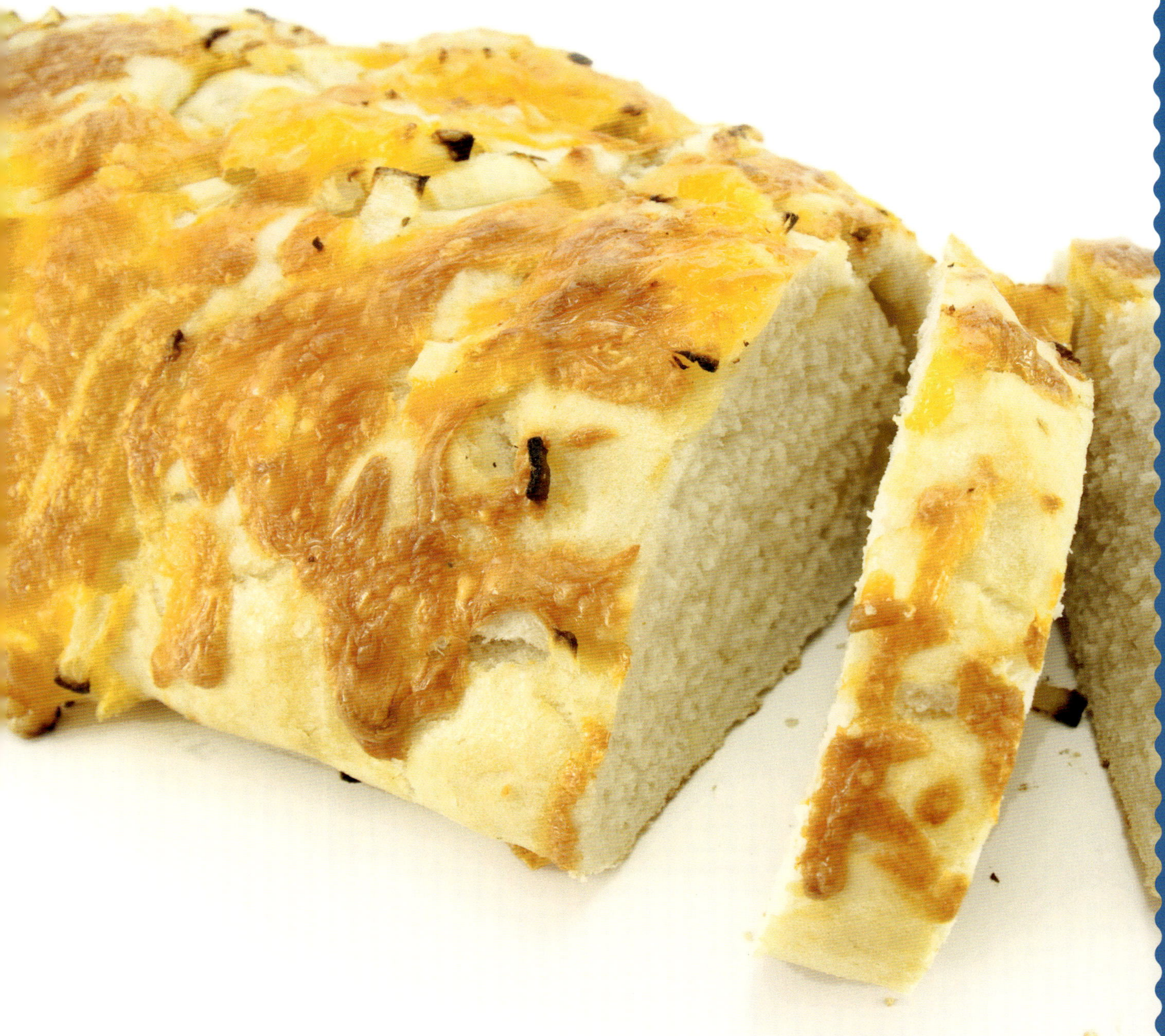

Brown Bread

BY BRIAN MCDERMOTT

8 SERVES   **10 MINUTES**   **40 MINUTES**

INGREDIENTS

125g plain flour
1 tsp bread soda
350g whole wheat flour
20g sugar
275ml buttermilk
150g natural yoghurt
1 egg
25g Donegal Rapeseed Oil

PREPARATION METHOD

Preheat the oven to 210°C.
Use a bowl and wooden spoon, do not use a mixer.
Sift the plain flour and bread soda, then add the whole wheat flour and sugar and mix thoroughly.

Beat the egg, Donegal Rapeseed Oil and yoghurt together.

Add buttermilk to make up 425ml. Add the liquid mixture to the dry flour mixture and mix together to form a deliberate wet mixture.

Grease two 1 lb loaf tins and drop mixture into tin half filling tin. Do not pat down mix as this tightens the resulting bread.

Bake in preheated oven at 210°C for 35 to 40 minutes. Allow to cool before slicing and serving.

This recipe may be used to make individual wheaten scones.

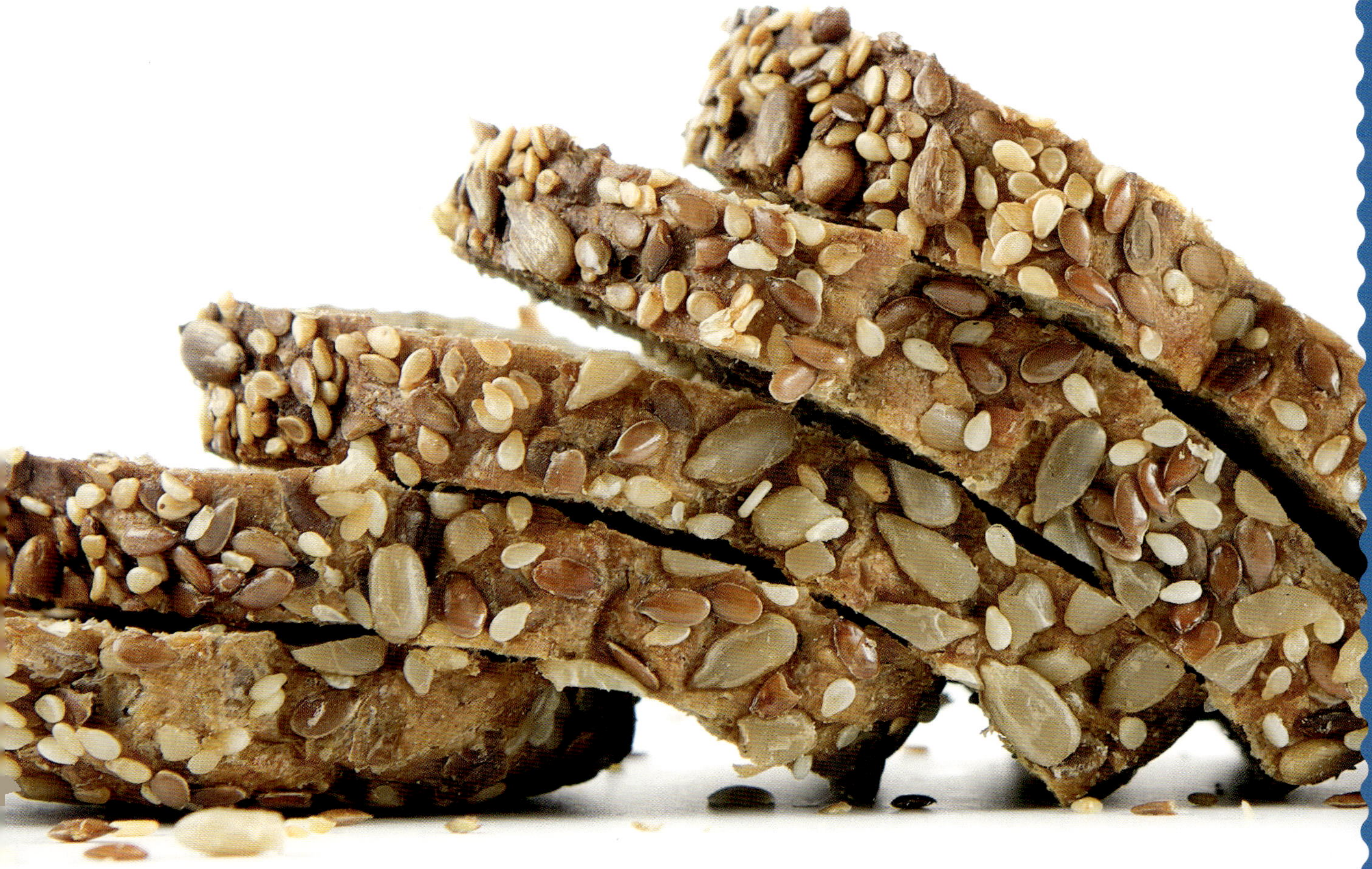

Wholegrain Cheese and Seed Bread

BY EIMEAR O'DONNELL

8 SERVES **10 MINUTES** **45 MINUTES**

INGREDIENTS

300g wholemeal flour
150g plain white flour
1 tsp bread soda, sifted
1 tsp salt
1 egg
370ml buttermilk, approx.
30g sesame seeds (plus a little extra for topping)
30g pumpkin seeds (plus a little extra for topping)
30g sunflower seeds
40g grated mature red cheddar
Sea salt and black pepper to season
1 tbsp Donegal Rapeseed Oil infused with Garlic

PREPARATION METHOD

Preheat the oven to 200°C or Gas Mark 6. Oil a Pyrex loaf tin using the Donegal Rapeseed Oil with Garlic.
Mix the flour, bread soda, seeds, cheese and salt together in a bowl.

Mix the egg with the buttermilk then mix into the flour. Add a little more buttermilk if the mixture is dry – the dough should be soft and sticky to touch.

Pour the mixture into the oiled loaf tin and sprinkle the remaining seeds on top.

Bake for 45 minutes.

Remove from the tin and wrap in a clean tea towel while cooling to keep the crust soft.

EIMEAR'S PASSION FOR FOOD LED HER TO A CAREER IN THE FOOD INDUSTRY. STUDYING A DEGREE IN FOOD SCIENCE FROM UNIVERSITY COLLEGE DUBLIN, EIMEAR HAS WORKED AS AN ANALYST IN THE FOOD SAFETY AUTHORITY OF IRELAND AND IS CURRENTLY WORKING AS A MARKETING SPECIALIST FOR KERRY, THE TASTE AND NUTRITION COMPANY. HER LOVE FOR QUALITY INGREDIENTS AND INTEREST IN NUTRITIONAL SCIENCE CAME FROM GROWING UP IN A HOME SURROUNDED BY HOME GROWN, HOMEMADE FOOD.

Banana and Walnut Bread

BY NIAMH MCATEER

8 SERVES   **20 MINUTES**   **45 MINUTES**

INGREDIENTS

2 ripe bananas
1 tsp bicarbonate of soda
½ cup natural yoghurt
¼ cup Donegal Rapeseed Oil
¾ cup light brown sugar
1 egg
1 tsp vanilla
1 cup plain flour
½ cup whole wheat flour
½ tsp cinnamon

PREPARATION METHOD

Line and grease a 1lb loaf tin.

Mash bananas, add the yogurt and bicarbonate of soda and let sit - you will see the mixture froth up, this will give the bread a light texture.

Whisk together the Donegal Rapeseed Oil, sugar, egg and vanilla.

Sift the flours, baking powder, cinnamon and salt.
Add the yoghurt mix and sugar mix to the flours and stir until just combined, then stir in the walnuts.

Tip into the lined and greased tin.

Bake at 180°C for 40 to 45 minutes.

BREAD AND BAKES

ORIGINALLY FROM GWEEDORE, CO. DONEGAL, LIVING IN DUBLIN FOR THE PAST 20 YEARS. I LEFT A CAREER IN IT IN 2005 TO OPEN DAISY CAKES BAKERY IN THE SOUTH DUBLIN SUBURB OF CHURCHTOWN. UNFORTUNATELY IN 2009 AS THE RECESSION TOOK HOLD I LOST THE BUSINESS. NOW BACK IN IT BUT STILL BAKING WHENEVER I CAN. WITH 3 KIDS (EWAN 12, ROAN 3 AND BREEGE 1) AND A FULL TIME JOB, I DON'T GET TO BAKE AS MUCH AS I'D LIKE BUT I'D NEVER LET A WEEK PASS WITHOUT BAKING. STILL IS AND ALWAYS WILL BE MY PASSION, MY STRESS RELIEVER, MY HAPPY PLACE.

Raspberry and Coconut Loaf

BY NIAMH MCATEER

8 SERVES — **15** MINUTES — **35** MINUTES

INGREDIENTS

3 bananas

2 eggs

100ml Donegal Rapeseed Oil

1 tbsp maple syrup

100g ground almonds

80g fine polenta

175g desiccated coconut

2 tsp baking powder

Zest of 1 lemon

Handful raspberries

PREPARATION METHOD

Mash bananas in a bowl, add eggs, Donegal Rapeseed Oil, maple syrup and zest, and whisk ingredients together.

Mix together the ground almonds, polenta, coconut and lemon zest.

Add wet to dry ingredients and stir until just combined. Stir in raspberries.

Grease and line a 1lb loaf tin.

Add some coconut on top of loaf for decoration and bake at 180°C for 30 to 35 minutes.

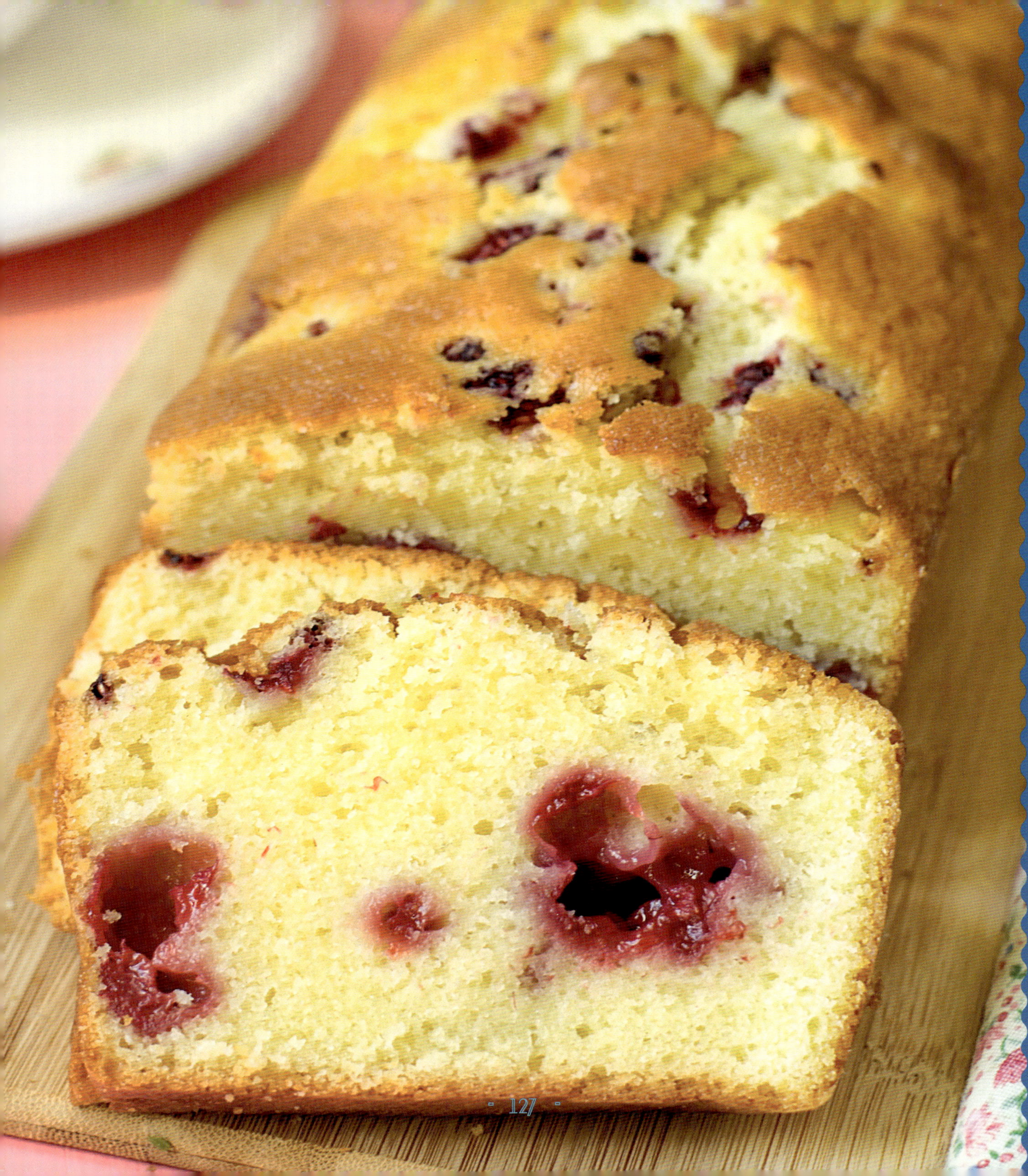

Carrot Cake

BY FOOD FOR THOUGHT, GALWAY

8 SERVES   **15** MINUTES   **90** MINUTES

INGREDIENTS

340g white self-raising flour
225g brown sugar
225g sultanas
½ tbsp ground cinnamon
1½ level tsp bread soda
1 fistful coconut
1 fistful of fresh grated carrot
4 pineapple rings, chopped in small pieces, no juice
5 free range eggs

PREPARATION METHOD

Place all the dry ingredients into a mixing bowl and add the pineapple, eggs and Donegal Rapeseed Oil. Mix together well with hands.

Grease bread tin and place the mixture in tin.

Cook at 160°C for 1 hour 30 mins

After first 40 minutes, check with skewer for consistency and cook for a remaining 50 minutes.

Allow to settle for 15 minutes once out of the oven. Turn upside down and tap out of tins.

FOOD FOR THOUGHT – VOTED GALWAY'S BEST CAFE – IS VERY POPULAR AMONG THE MORE HEALTH-CONSCIENCE, AS WELL AS THOSE LOOKING FOR A GREAT VALUE EATERY. A FRIENDLY, FAMILY-RUN CAFE SERVING FRESH, HOME BAKED FOOD AND A CULT FAVORITE IN GALWAY.

Chocolate Cake

8 SERVES | 20 MINUTES | 35 MINUTES

INGREDIENTS

225g plain flour
350g caster sugar
85g cocoa powder
1½ tsp baking powder
1½ tsp bicarbonate of soda
2 free range eggs
250ml milk
125ml Donegal Rapeseed Oil
2 tsp vanilla extract
250ml boiling water

Chocolate Icing

200g plain chocolate
200ml double cream

PREPARATION METHOD

Preheat the oven to 180°C or Gas Mark 4. Grease and line two 20cm or 8 inch sandwich tins.

Place all of the cake ingredients, except the boiling water, into a large mixing bowl. Using a wooden spoon, or electric whisk, beat the mixture until smooth and well combined.

Add the boiling water to the mixture, a little at a time, until smooth.

Divide the cake batter between the sandwich tins and bake in the oven for 25-35 minutes, or until the top is firm to the touch and a skewer inserted into the centre of the cake comes out clean.

Remove the cakes from the oven and allow to cool completely in their tins before icing.

For the chocolate icing, heat the chocolate and cream in a saucepan over a low heat until the chocolate melts. Remove the pan from the heat and whisk the mixture until smooth and thickened. Set aside to cool for 1-2 hours.

To assemble the cake, run a knife around the inside of the cake tins to loosen the cakes. Carefully remove the cakes from the tins.

Spread a little chocolate icing over the top of one of the chocolate cakes, then carefully place the other chocolate cake on top of it. Transfer the cake to a serving plate and ice the cake all over with the chocolate icing, using a palette knife.

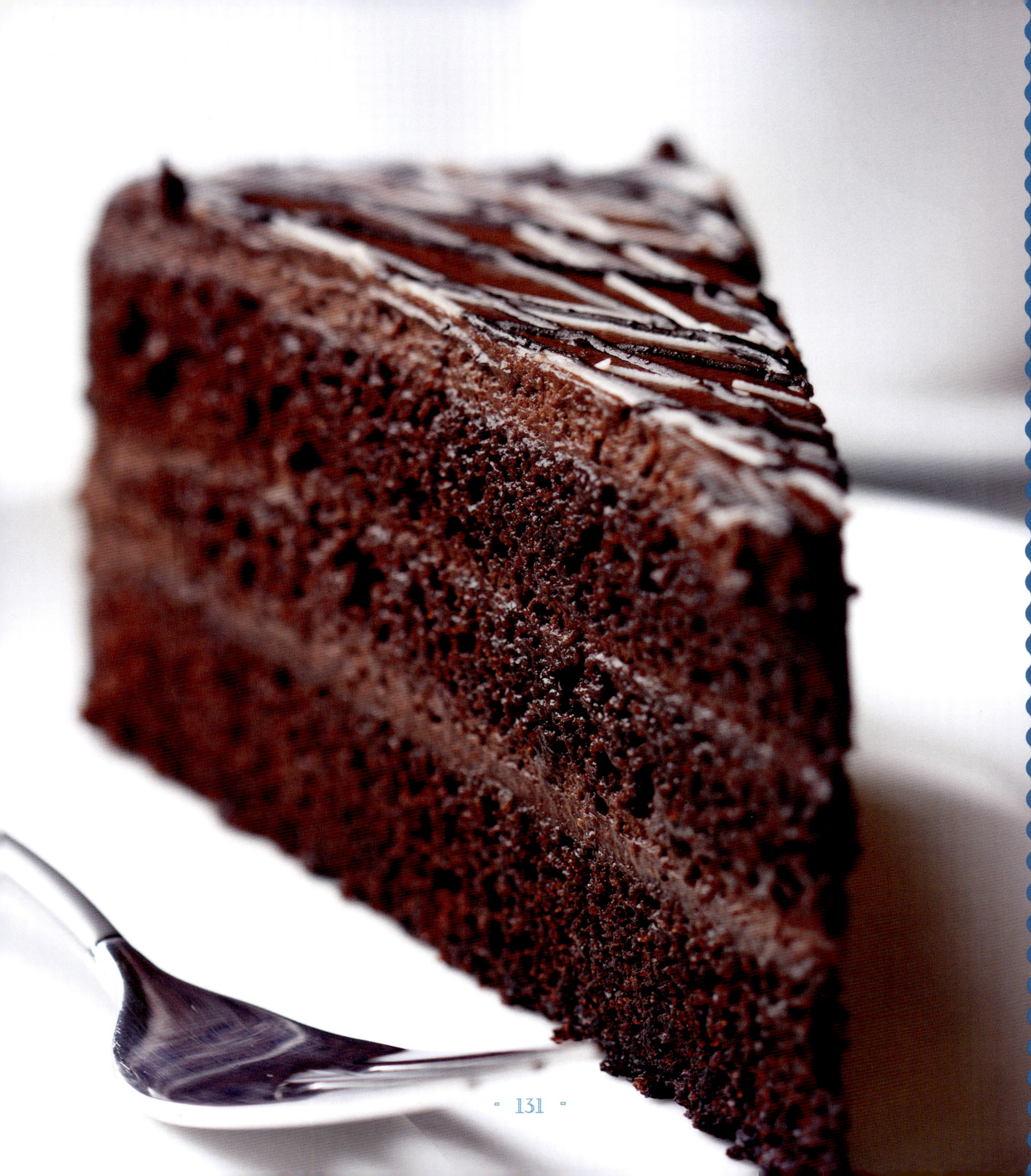

Apple and Donegal Rapeseed Oil Cake

BY SHELLS CAFÉ
WWW.SHELLSCAFE.COM

8 SERVES | 30 MINUTES | 45 MINUTES

INGREDIENTS

200g golden caster sugar

3 large eggs

150ml Donegal Rapeseed Oil

350g flour

½ tsp ground ginger

1 tsp ground cinnamon

1 tsp bicarbonate of soda (bread soda)

1 tsp baking powder

110g golden raisins or sultanas

80g walnuts, crushed

Pinch of salt

Grated zest of lemon

2 cooking apples, grated

Honey Cream Cheese Frosting

120g cream cheese

2 tbsp honey

PREPARATION METHOD

Preheat the oven to 180°C or 350°F.

Place the sultanas or raisins in a bowl of hot water and allow to soak for 15 minutes to plump up.

Whisk the sugar and eggs until doubled in volume and pale cream in colour. Warm the Donegal Rapeseed Oil and slowly whisk in with the eggs and sugar.

Sieve the flour, cinnamon, ginger, bread soda, salt and baking powder together. Then gradually add in to the oil and sugar mixture. Fold in well.

Drain the raisins or sultanas from the water and add to the mixture along with the lemon zest, crushed walnuts and grated apples. Mix thoroughly. The mixture should be stiff at this stage.

Butter and flour a 20cm spring form cake tin and spoon in the mixture. Bake for about 45 minutes until a skewer placed in the middle comes out dry.

Carefully remove the cake from the tin and allow to cool on a wire rack.

Honey Cream Cheese Frosting: Whisk the cream cheese and honey together and spread evenly onto the cake once it has cooled.

A SURFER'S HAVEN, SHELLS CAFÉ IS LOCATED RIGHT ON THE BEACH IN STRANDHILL, CO SLIGO. WINNER OF THE BEST FLAT WHITE IN IRELAND, THIS CAFE DOES EVERYTHING JUST RIGHT. FROM HOME BAKED BREADS AND CAKES TO THE BEST FISH AND CHIPS- SHELLS CAFÉ IS THE PLACE TO BE.

Donegal Rapeseed Oil, Orange & Rosemary Polenta Cake

BY CHEF SHANE SMITH
WWW.CHEFSHANESMITH.IE

10 SERVES **20 MINUTES** **50 MINUTES**

INGREDIENTS

125ml Donegal Rapeseed Oil infused with Lemon
150g coarse polenta
75g plain flour
½ tsp baking powder
150g caster sugar
2 large eggs
2 egg whites
250g yoghurt
Zest & juice of 1 medium orange

Soaking syrup

125g caster sugar
180ml orange juice
1 tsp chopped rosemary

PREPARATION METHOD

Preheat the oven to 160°C.

Grease and line a 20cm loose bottom cake tin.

In a bowl whisk the sugar, eggs and whites until thick and pale in colour.

In a separate bowl, mix the flour, polenta and baking powder.

Add the Donegal Rapeseed Oil infused with Lemon and yoghurt to the egg mixture and mix.

Add in the dry ingredients and fold to incorporate.

Pour the batter into the lined tin and bake in the centre of the oven for 45-50 minutes.

When this is baking, place all the ingredients for the soaking liquid into a pot and heat gently until the sugar has dissolved, set aside.

Once the cake is baked, remove from the oven and place on a cooling rack, strain the liquid and spoon over the cake in stages until it is all soaked in.

Top with some orange zest and rosemary sprigs.
Serve with a spoon of natural yoghurt.
Enjoy!

[M]ASTER PASTRY CHEF, SHANE SMITH HAS NEARLY 20 YEARS OF [E]XPERIENCE WORKING IN SOME OF THE WORLD'S MOST CELEBRATED [P]ASTRY KITCHENS ACROSS THE GLOBE. THE CAVAN NATIVE IS HEAD PASTRY [C]HEF AND HEAD OF PRODUCT DEVELOPMENT AT AIRFIELD ESTATE IN [DU]NDRUM.
[H]E IS A REGULAR CONTRIBUTOR TO THETASTE.IE, SHANE ALSO WRITES A [M]ONTHLY COLUMN FOR THE ANGLO CELT NEWSPAPER.
[TH]E ASPIRING CHEF BEGAN HIS FORMAL TRAINING AT KILLYBEGS TOURISM [C]OLLEGE IN DONEGAL, AND WENT ON TO GRADUATE WITH A DEGREE IN [C]ULINARY ARTS, SPECIALISING IN PASTRY, FROM GALWAY-MAYO INSTITUTE [OF] TECHNOLOGY.
[IN] SEPTEMBER 2015, SHANE WAS AWARDED THE TITLE OF BEST BAKERY [M]ANAGER IN IRELAND IN CONJUNCTION WITH SHELFLIFE MAGAZINE. SHANE [AL]SO HAS A REGULAR COOKERY SLOT ON SUNDAY AM, TV3.

Strawberry Muffins

12 SERVES   **15** MINUTES   **25** MINUTES

INGREDIENTS

280g flour
2 tbsp sweetener
1 tbsp baking powder
250g fresh strawberries, chopped
2 eggs, lightly beaten
120ml low fat milk
115g light sour cream
80ml Donegal Rapeseed Oil

Topping

30g flour
1 tbsp sweetener
½ tsp ground cinnamon
15g cold sunflower margarine

PREPARATION METHOD

Preheat the oven to 220°C or Gas Mark 7 and line a 12 cup muffin tin with paper cups.

Combine the flour, sweetener and baking powder in a large bowl. Fold in the strawberries.

Whisk together the eggs, milk, sour cream and Donegal Rapeseed Oil. Stir into the dry ingredients until just combined.

For the topping combine the flour, sweetener and cinnamon in a small bowl. Rub in the margarine until crumbly.

Fill the muffin cups about two thirds full and top with the streusel topping. Bake for 20-25 minutes until a skewer inserted into the centre comes out clean.

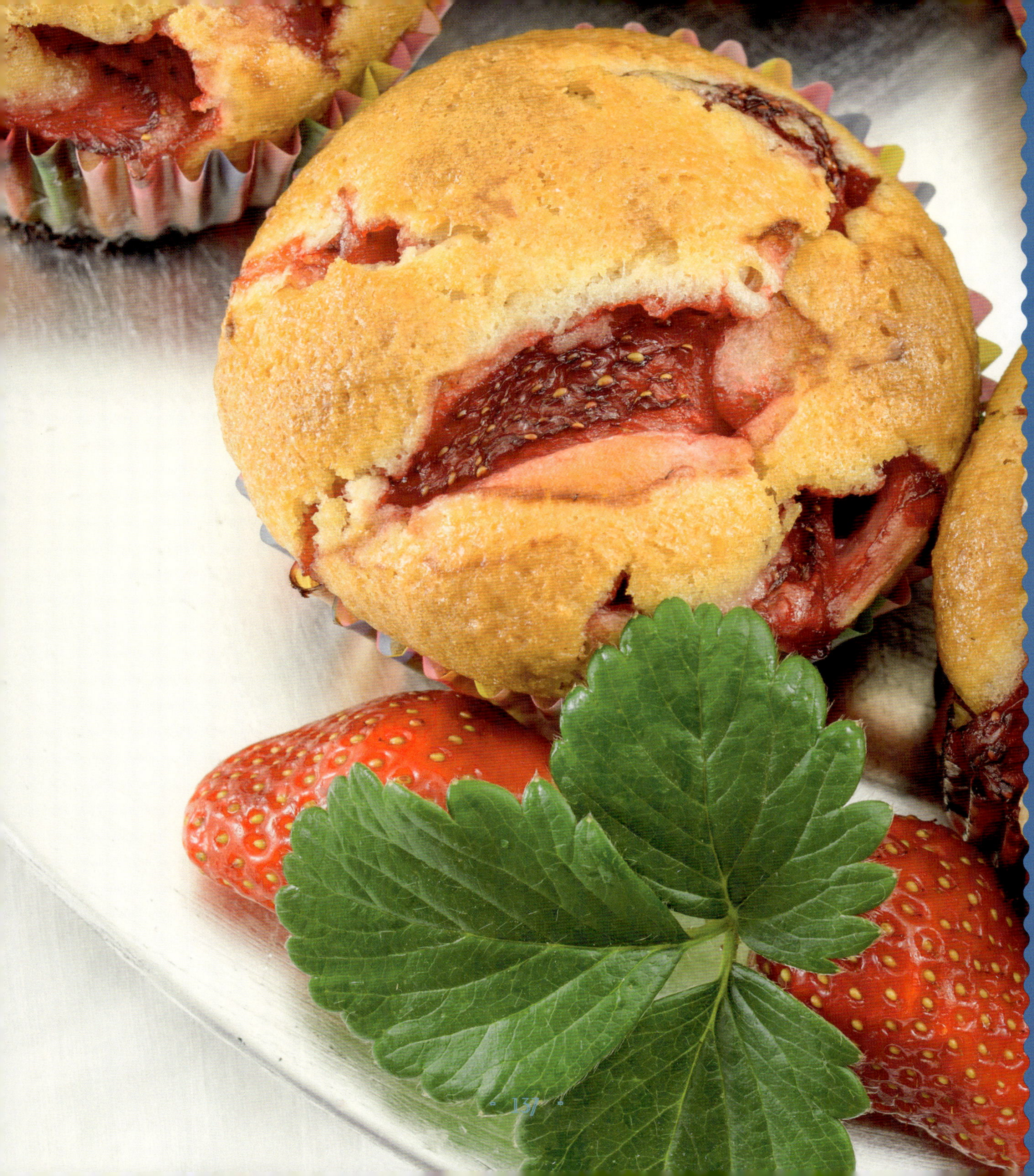

Baked potato with grated cheddar and Ballymaloe Relish

BY BALLYMALOE FOODS
WWW.BALLYMALOEFOODS.COM

SERVES 1
MINUTES 5
MINUTES 60

INGREDIENTS

A large potato, (Golden Wonder or Records are good)
Donegal Rapeseed Oil
Salt and pepper
A hand full of grated cheddar
A sprinkle of finely sliced spring onions
Ballymaloe Relish
Balsamic Vinegar
Fresh green leaves

PREPARATION METHOD

A baked potato is easy peasy to do. So for those who can't cook at all, this is a good one to start with.

It's this simple: turn on the oven to 180ºC or Gas Mark 4. Scrub the potato, prick it with a knife and put it in the oven.

Wait for about an hour (this depends on the size of the spud) and when it's soft in the centre its ready.

With the point of a sharp knife cut a large cross, a few centimetres deep, on the top.

Open the potato on a plate, season with a sprinkle of salt and pepper, add a knob of butter, sprinkle with a little cheddar cheese and spring onions, and pop a spoon of Ballymaloe Relish on top.

Serve with a green salad drizzled with Donegal Rapeseed Oil and a little Balsamic Vinegar. That's it!

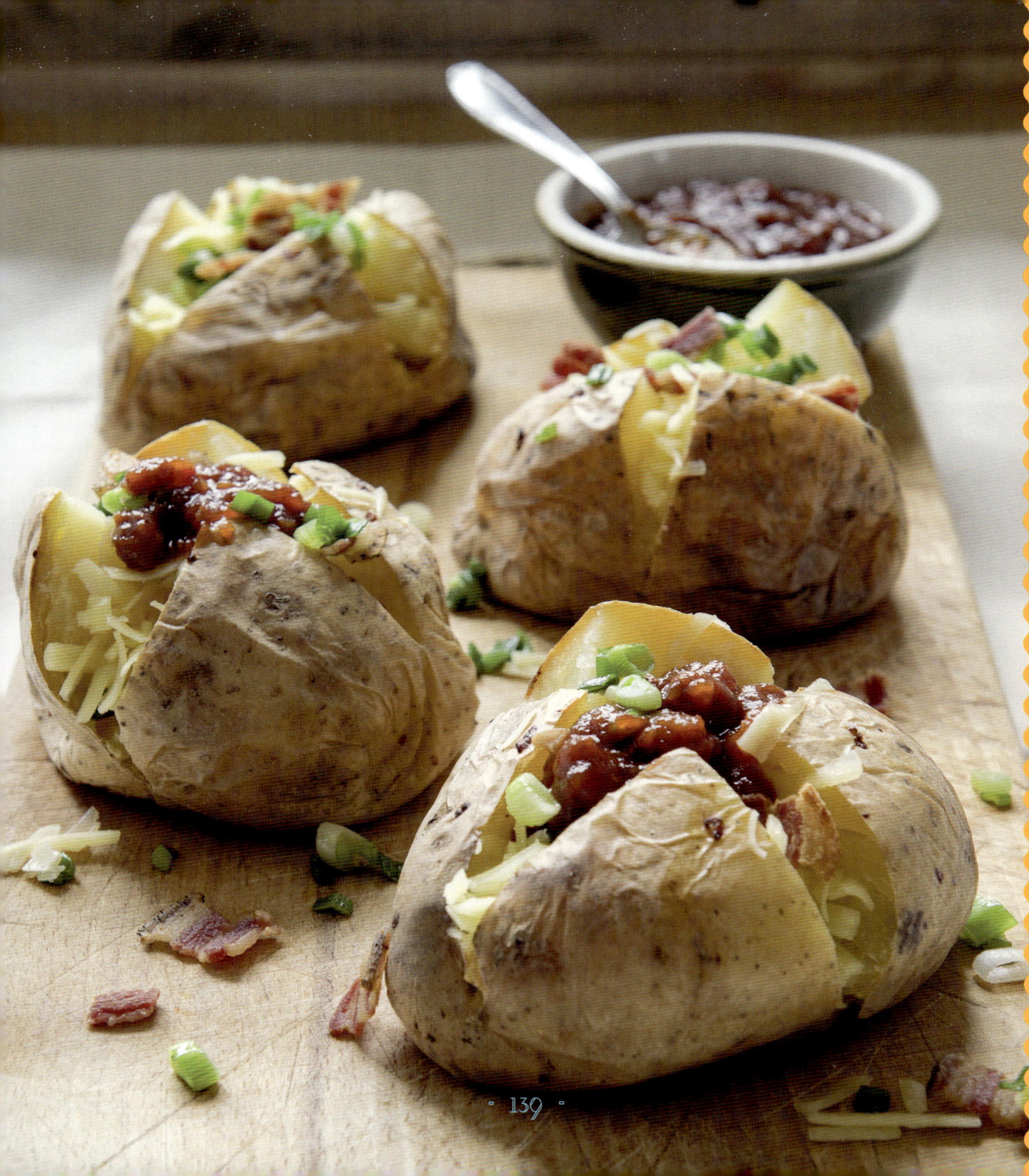

Three Cheese Chorizo

BY CARL MARK O'NEILL
WWW.IRELANDSTABLEPRODUCE.COM

1 SERVES · **10 MINUTES** · **-**

INGREDIENTS

Despard Bread -supplied by Bretzel Bakery, Portobello
Rocket leaves -from McCormack's Farm
Red oak leaves -from McCormack's Farm
Gubbeen smoked chorizo, sliced
St Tola pure Irish goat cheese
Cahill's Farm Irish cheddar with chives
Mossfield Organic Slieve Bloom
Cherry vine tomatoes, sliced -grown by Foley's Farm, North Dublin
Cucumber, finely sliced -supplied by Matt Butler's Fruit Market, Smithfield
Pinch Oriel sea salt
Donegal Rapeseed Oil Honey and Mustard Dressing, for drizzling

PREPARATION METHOD

The Despard Bread is an alternative to your everyday French stick. Made from scratch by the Bretzel Bakery Portobello Dublin, it is freshly baked and delivered to local artisan shops, cafes and restaurants across Dublin.

Start by slicing the Despard bread and gently placing a bed of Mc Cormack's Farm rocket and red oak leaves on top.
Add sliced Gubbeen smoked chorizo and sliced cherry vine tomatoes.

Add some of Ireland's Finest Farmhouse cheeses; Mossfield Organic Slieve Bloom, Cahills Farm Irish cheddar with chive, St Tola pure Irish goat cheese. Thinly slice cucumber and add. Season with a pinch of Oriel sea salt.
Drizzle with Donegal Rapeseed Oil Honey and Mustard Dressing and enjoy.

My name is Carl Mark O'Neill and I have worked in retail trade for the best part of thirty years -in Superquinn, Donnybrook Fair, Supervalu, Spar and Morton's of Ranelagh- allowing me to gain a unique insight into the quality of locally produced artisan food and beverages in Ireland. I have always been interested in photography as well. In 2011 the idea to combine my two passions led me on a photographic journey, capturing the individual stories of food production and bringing them into the public eye, having a look at the various producers and admiring the stages that the various products go through. I launched my website in 2011: www.irelandstableproduce.com. I was also a food and beverage columnist for Travel Ireland Magazine, food styling and doing photography, from June 2016 to February 2017.

Bacon 'n' Egg Muffins

BY EMMET RUSHE - RUSHE FITNESS
WWW.RUSHEFITNESS.IE

1 SERVES   **10** MINUTES   **15** MINUTES

INGREDIENTS

6 eggs
2 rashers of bacon
1 small onion, finely diced
1 tsp dried oregano
½ tsp of chilli powder
1 tbsp Donegal Rapeseed Oil

PREPARATION METHOD

Preheat oven to 180°C or Gas Mark 4 and line a muffin tin with 4 paper cases.

In a bowl whisk the eggs and seasoning together.
In a small frying pan, using the Donegal Rapeseed oil, fry the bacon until crispy.
Allow to cool slightly, then chop or crumble the bacon.
Add the bacon and onion to the egg mix. Beat well and divide between the 4 muffin cases.

Bake in the oven for 10 to 15 minutes until firm.

These savoury muffins can be eaten chilled and taken to work in lunchboxes also.

EVERYTHING WE DO AT RUSHE FITNESS IS BUILT AROUND THE PEOPLE WHO TRAIN WITH US.
WHETHER IT IS GROUP TRAINING IN OUR FIT IN 42 PROGRAM, 1-1 PERSONAL TRAINING, OR THROUGH OUR BESPOKE ONLINE TRAINING PACKAGES, WE HELP OUR MEMBERS TO ACHIEVE THEIR DESIRED RESULTS IN A FUN AND SUPPORTIVE ENVIRONMENT

Poached Egg on Sourdough Bruschetta

2 SERVES   10 MINUTES   20 MINUTES

INGREDIENTS

Hollandaise Sauce

150g unsalted butter
2 egg yolks
½ tsp white wine vinegar
1 tbsp cold water
Sea salt and freshly ground black pepper
4 tbsp Donegal Rapeseed Oil infused with White Truffle

Bruschetta

4 slices of sourdough loaf or other crusty bread
4 tbsp Donegal Rapeseed Oil
4 free range eggs
8-10 asparagus tips, cooked in boiling water and cooled

PREPARATION METHOD

First make the hollandaise sauce. Melt the butter in a saucepan, allow to cool and skim any white solids from surface. Keep the butter warm. Put the egg yolks, white wine vinegar, water and a little salt and pepper in a heat proof bowl that will fit over a small pan. Whisk together.

Put the bowl over a pan of barely simmering water and whisk continuously until pale and thick, about 3-4 minutes.

Remove from the heat and slowly whisk in the melted butter, a little at a time until it's all incorporated and you have a thick and creamy hollandaise. If it gets too thick, add a splash of water.

Whisk in the Donegal Rapeseed Oil infused with White Truffle, a tbsp at a time.

Now make the bruschetta. Preheat a griddle pan over a high heat. Brush each side of the bread with Donegal Rapeseed Oil. Place the bread on the pan and chargrill the bread on one side until it is nicely charred and a little bit crispy. Turn the bread over and then char on the other side. Set aside.

Place the cooked asparagus on the griddle pan to warm through.

Now poach your eggs in simmering water to your liking.

To serve, top the bruschetta with the poached eggs and asparagus. Spoon over the white truffle hollandaise.

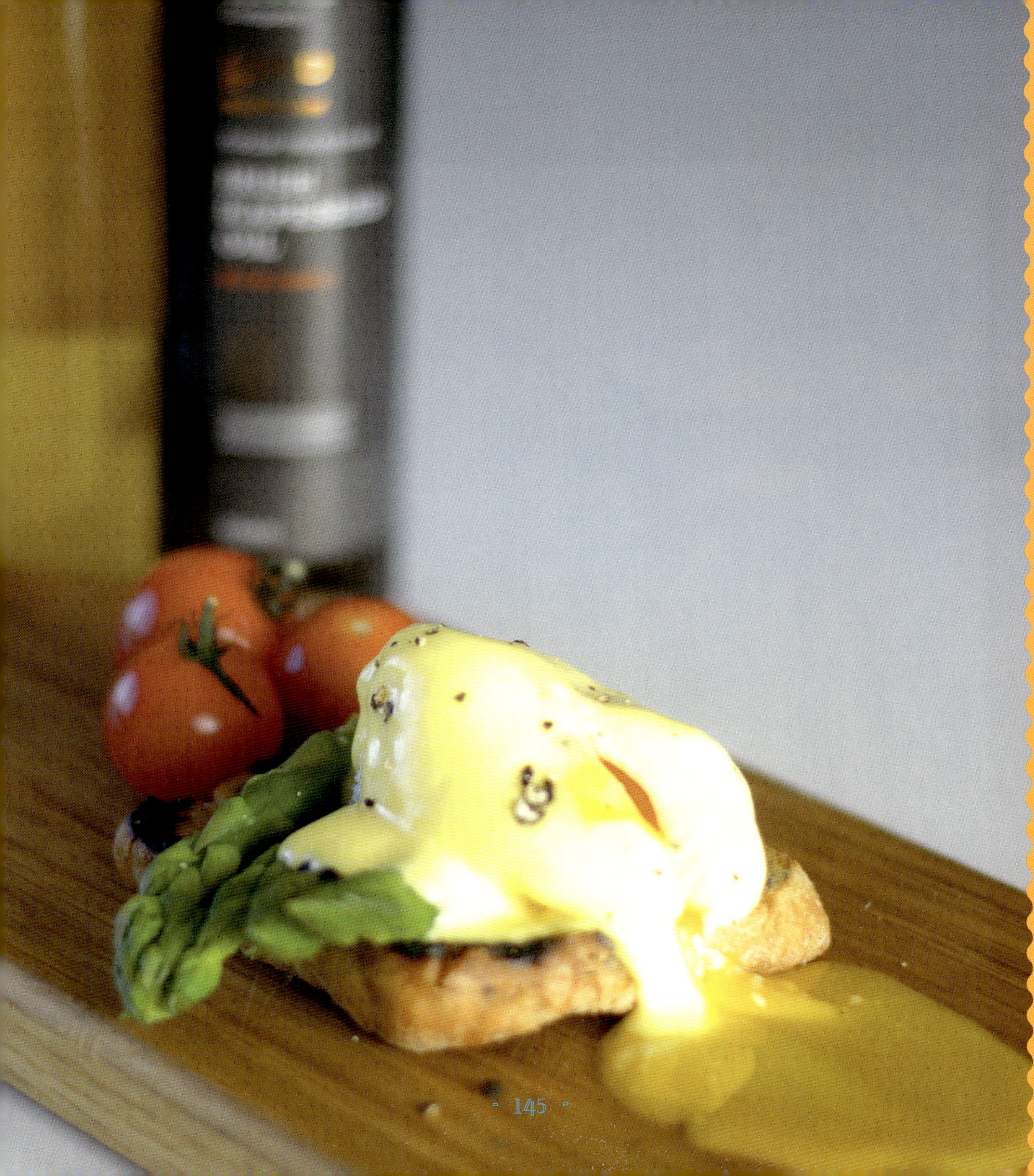

Shakshuka

BY ANNA-JANE KINGSTON
WWW.THYMETOEAT.IE

2-4 SERVES **10 MINUTES** **30 MINUTES**

INGREDIENTS

2 tbsp of Donegal Rapeseed Oil infused with Garlic
4 large eggs
1 red bell pepper
½ courgette
1 can chopped tomatoes
2 tbsp tomato purée
¼ cup water
1 tbsp cumin
1½ tsp paprika or smoked paprika
½ tsp cayenne or chilli powder
Salt and black pepper
½ tsp sugar
2 tbsp freshly chopped coriander
½ can kidney beans or ½ can cannelloni/butter beans, drained and rinsed

PREPARATION METHOD

Dice up the pepper and courgette.

Gently heat the Donegal Rapeseed Oil infused with Garlic on a medium to high heat in a large frying pan or skillet. Add the courgette and pepper and sauté for about 5 minutes.

Add all the dry spices and continue to cook for a further two minutes, stirring constantly.

Add in the tin of chopped tomatoes, the tomato purée, the sugar and the water. Lower the temperature to a simmering heat and allow the mixture to reduce and thicken for about ten minutes. Taste and season at this point too with some of the fresh coriander, salt and pepper.

One by one, make little wells in the mixture with a spoon and crack an egg into each one.

Leave the mixture for about 10-15 minutes depending on how you like your eggs. 10 minutes will give you nice runny yolks.

Sprinkle the rest of the fresh coriander over the Shakshuka and serve with some ciabatta or sourdough bread to mop up the tasty sauce.

LUNCH AND LITE BITES

ANNA-JANE KINGSTON IS THE WRITER AND CREATOR OF THE SUCCESSFUL FOOD BLOG THYMETOEAT.IE. SINCE SETTING UP THE BLOG IN 2015, ANNA-JANE'S CULINARY TALENTS HAVE SEEN HER BEING INVITED TO DO DEMOS ON THE POPULAR IRELAND AM COOKERY SLOT, FEATURE IN MANY OF IRELAND'S TOP FOOD MAGAZINES AND ALSO STARRING AS A GUEST DINER ON TV3'S THE RESTAURANT. BRIMMING WITH MOUTH-WATERING FOOD PHOTOGRAPHY, HER WEBSITE MAINLY FOCUSES ON HEALTHY EATING, WITH SIMPLE AND CREATIVE RECIPES SUITABLE FOR ALL TYPES OF EATERS.

Huevos Rancheros

BY I LOVE COOKING
WWW.ILOVECOOKING.IE

4 SERVES   **5 MINUTES**   **25 MINUTES**

INGREDIENTS

- 3 tbsp Donegal Rapeseed Oil
- 1 medium red onion, sliced
- 1 tsp smoked paprika
- 1 red pepper, sliced into strips
- 1 yellow pepper, sliced into strips
- 1 red chilli, sliced
- 2 garlic cloves, finely minced
- 2 tins tomato
- Salt and pepper
- 4 eggs

To Serve

- Strong cheddar cheese, grated
- Fresh coriander

PREPARATION METHOD

Heat a large pan on medium heat with the Donegal Rapeseed Oil. Once hot, add the onion and paprika and cook until onion begins to soften. Add the peppers, chilli and garlic and cook for a further 5 minutes.

Increase heat to medium high and add the tins of tomato and bring to a boil, then reduce heat and leave to simmer until tomato sauce has thickened, about 15 minutes, stirring occasionally.

Use the back of a large spoon or ladle to create 4 wells in the tomato sauce, then carefully crack an egg into each well. Place a lid over the pan leaving a gap for steam to escape, and leave eggs to poach for about 5 minutes or until the tops of the eggs are just set.

Remove from heat and scatter generously with cheese and coriander then serve at the table straight from the pan.

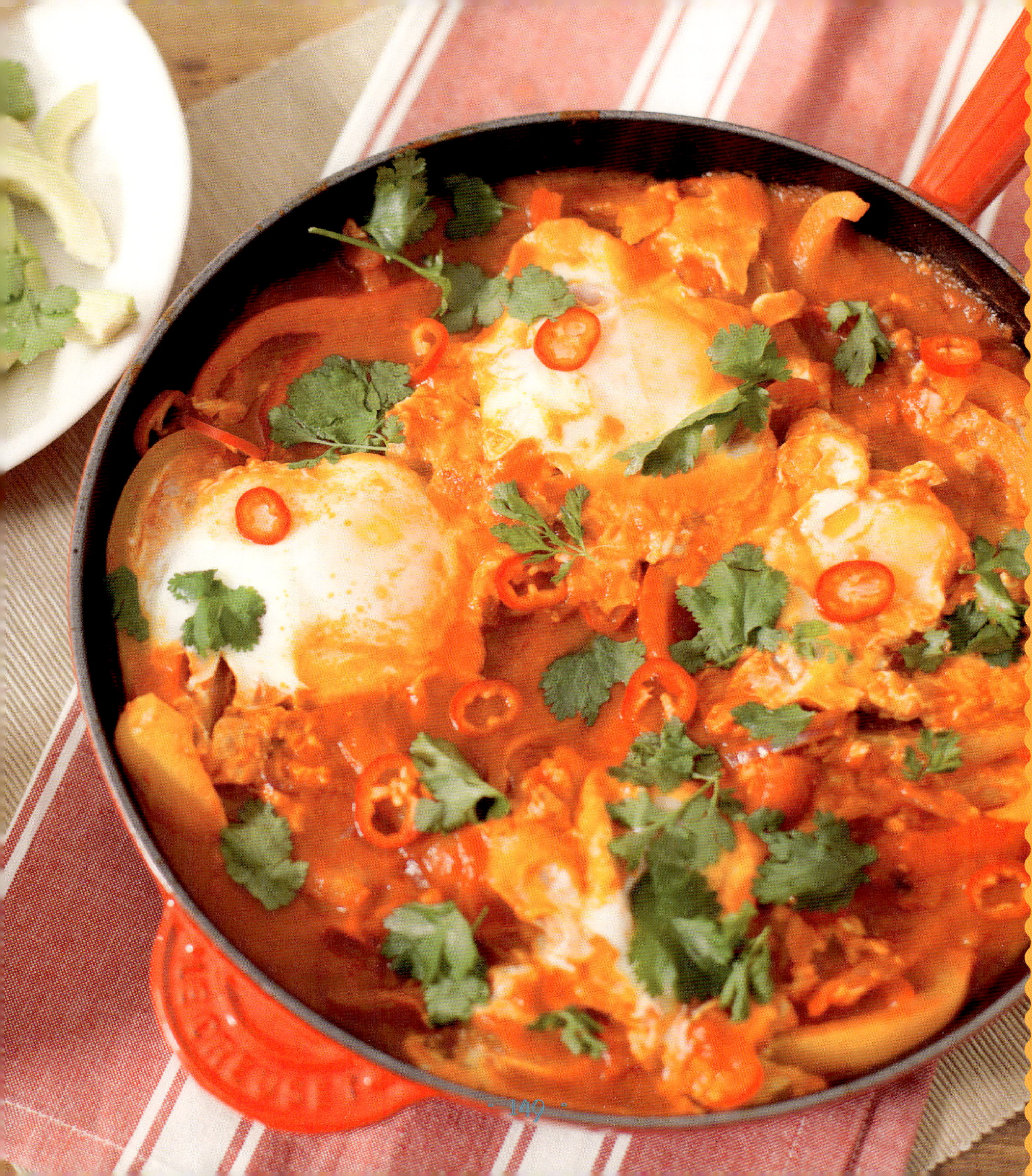

Hummus with Garlic, Chilli and Parmesan

BY EIMEAR O'DONNELL

2 SERVES · 5 MINUTES · -

INGREDIENTS

2 tins of chickpeas
3 tbsp garlic purée
¼ cup Donegal Rapeseed Oil infused with Lemon
¼ cup tahini
¼ cup parmesan cheese, grated
1 tbsp ground black peppercorns
1 tsp ground coriander
Juice of 1 lemon
2 tbsp chilli flakes
Sea salt
Sprig of fresh parsley, finely chopped

PREPARATION METHOD

Drain the chickpeas and wash under cold water. Blend in the food processor until mashed.

Add the garlic, Donegal Rapeseed Oil infused with Lemon, tahini, cheese, pepper, coriander, lemon juice, and chilli and blend until fully incorporated.

Season with sea salt to taste and add additional lemon or chilli if the taste is still bland.

Serve with fresh parsley sprinkled on top.

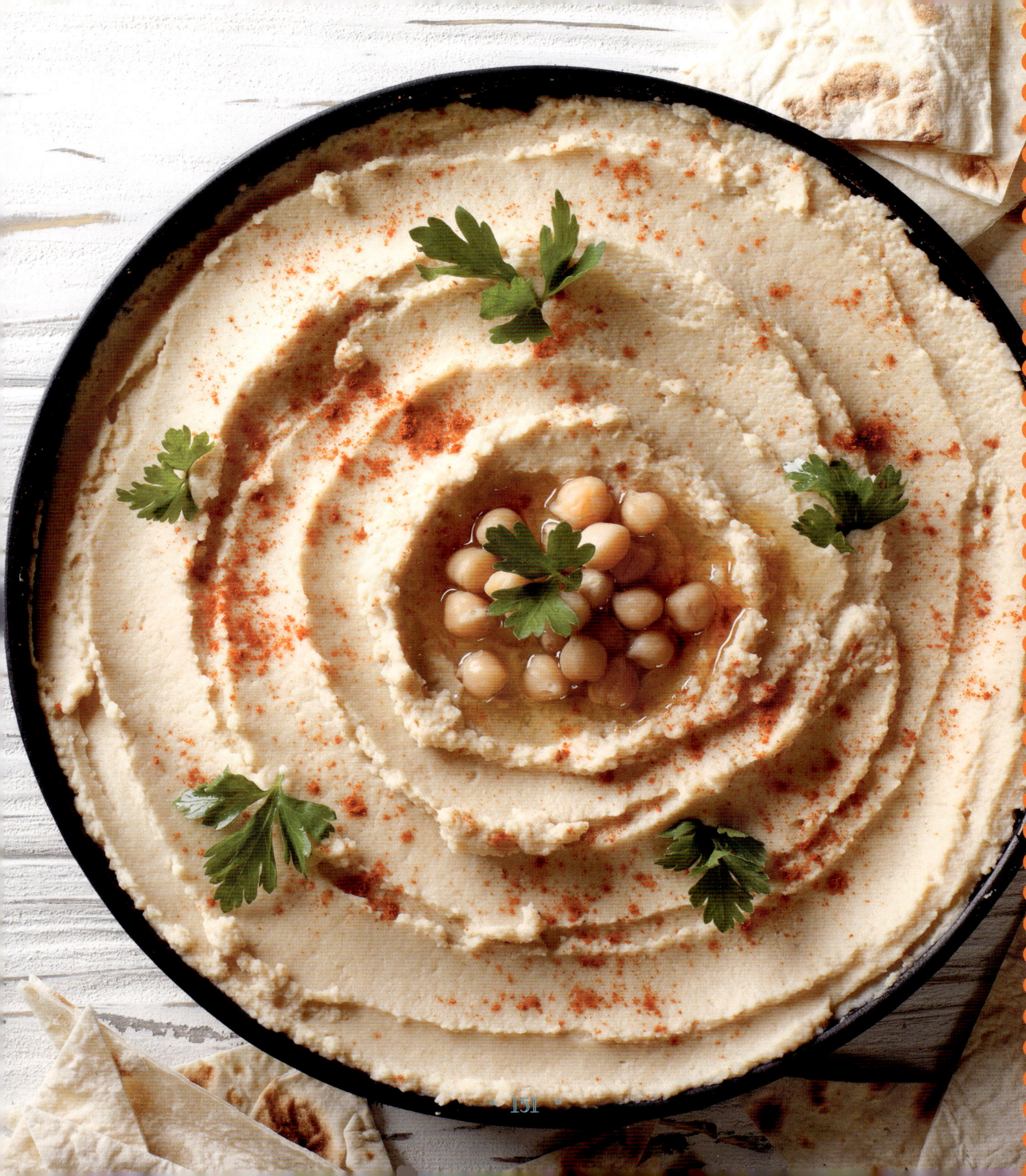

Crushed Chickpeas

INGREDIENTS

400g tin of cooked chickpeas
1 tsp of cumin seeds
½ red chilli, finely chopped
½ clove of garlic, crushed
Juice of ½ lemon
Sea salt & pepper, to taste
2 tbsp Donegal Rapeseed Oil

PREPARATION METHOD

Place all of the above in a food processor or blender, and pulse to a coarse pulp.

Semi Dried Cherry Tomato Salsa

INGREDIENTS

Punnet of cherry or plum tomatoes
1 clove of garlic, thinly sliced
1 white onion, thinly sliced
Pinch of sugar
Donegal Rapeseed Oil

PREPARATION METHOD

Half the tomatoes if big, toss with the onion, garlic and sugar in Donegal Rapeseed Oil.
Spread on a baking sheet and place under the grill until roasted, toss and do not allow to burn. This should only take a few minutes.

Curry and Mango Dip

INGREDIENTS

3 tbsp mango chutney
Juice of ½ lime
2 spring onions, chopped
80g cream cheese
125g Greek yoghurt
2 tbsp Donegal Rapeseed Oil infused with Curry

PREPARATION METHOD

Place all ingredients into a bowl and mix well until blended.

DRESSING AND DIPS

Guacamole

INGREDIENTS

3 avocados
Juice of 1 lime
1 tsp salt
½ onion, diced
Handful fresh coriander, chopped
2 plum tomatoes, diced
1 clove garlic, minced
1 pinch ground cayenne pepper (optional)
Donegal Rapeseed Oil, to drizzle

PREPARATION METHOD

Peel the avocados and remove the stones.
Mash together the avocados, lime juice and salt.
Add in the onion, coriander, tomatoes, garlic and cayenne pepper and mix well.
Drizzle some Donegal Rapeseed Oil on top of the guacamole before serving.
Can be served immediately. For best results refrigerate for 1 hour.

Sundried Tomato Pesto

INGREDIENTS

175g semi sundried tomatoes, roughly chopped
8 large fresh basil leaves
2 garlic cloves, peeled
200ml Donegal Rapeseed Oil
Sea salt and freshly ground black pepper

PREPARATION METHOD

Place the semi sundried tomatoes in a food processor or blender with the basil leaves and garlic and pulse to finely chop.
Switch the machine back on and slowly pour in the oil through the feeder tube until the pesto has emulsified.
Transfer to a bowl with a spatula and season to taste.

Garlic Pesto

INGREDIENTS

50g wild garlic
6 tbsp Donegal Rapeseed Oil
70g pine nuts
70g parmesan cheese
½ tsp sea salt
½ tsp crushed black pepper

PREPARATION METHOD

Blitz everything together in a food processor or bullet. Add extra salt, pepper and parmesan depending on your flavour preference.

Hidden Veggie Tomato Sauce
BY I LOVE COOKING

INGREDIENTS

1 tbsp Donegal Rapeseed Oil
1 red onion, roughly chopped
2 cloves garlic, roughly chopped
2 carrots, chopped
1 courgette, chopped
1 celery stick, chopped
20g baby spinach leaves
500g passata
1 x 400g tin whole peeled tomatoes
1 vegetable stock cube
1 tbsp dried mixed herbs
1 tsp paprika
1 tsp salt
½ tsp black pepper

PREPARATION METHOD

Heat a large saucepan or pot over medium heat. Add the Donegal Rapeseed Oil, onion and garlic and fry for 2-3 minutes until soft. Add the chopped carrots, courgette, celery and spinach, give a quick stir to mix.

Pour in the passata and tinned tomato along with the stock cube and stir well. Add the dried herbs, salt, paprika and pepper and bring to a boil. Lower heat to medium low and leave to simmer for at least 20 minutes.

Allow the sauce to cool then liquidise using a blender until it is smooth.

The sauce can be used straight away or poured into jars and stored in the fridge for up to 1 week. It can also be divided into freezer safe containers and frozen for up to 3 months.

Honey and Rapeseed Oil Dressing

BY GARY STAFFORD - LYONS CAFE
WWW.LYONSCAFE.COM

INGREDIENTS

- 2 tbsp Dijon mustard
- 4 tbsp white wine vinegar
- 3 tbsp honey
- 400ml Donegal Rapeseed Oil
- Sea salt and ground black pepper, to taste

PREPARATION METHOD

Using a whisk, combine mustard, vinegar, and honey in a mixing bowl. Whilst whisking, slowly add the Donegal Rapeseed Oil until a thick emulsion is achieved.

If dressing appears to separate, chill for around 10 minutes and re-whisk. Taste and season accordingly.

This dressing keeps for up to a month in the fridge.

THIS RECIPE WILL PRODUCE AROUND 600ML OF A DRESSING THAT'S VERY VERSATILE. IT'S GREAT ON GREEN LEAVES OR TO TOSS ROASTED VEG IN AS A SALAD DISH.

MARINADES

Garlic and Herb Marinade

INGREDIENTS

75ml Donegal Rapeseed Oil
75ml water
75ml vinegar
3 cloves garlic, finely chopped
1 tsp dried thyme
1 tsp dried Italian herb seasoning
1 tsp chicken seasoning

PREPARATION METHOD

Mix all ingredients together in a bowl and apply to meat.

8 SERVES

Steak Marinade

INGREDIENTS

4 tbsp Donegal Rapeseed Oil
4 tbsp balsamic vinegar
4 tbsp Worcestershire sauce
4 tbsp soy sauce
2 tsp Dijon mustard
2 tsp minced garlic
Salt and pepper, to taste

PREPARATION METHOD

Mix all ingredients together in a bowl and apply to meat.

4 SERVES

Kebab Marinade

INGREDIENTS

175g honey
125ml soy sauce
4 tbsp tomato based chilli sauce
1 tbsp ground cumin, to taste
2 tbsp Donegal Rapeseed oil

PREPARATION METHOD

Whisk all ingredients together until combined and apply to meat.
Ideal for chicken, pork and vegetable kebabs.

4 SERVES

Citrus and Garlic Prawn Marinade

INGREDIENTS

110ml Donegal Rapeseed Oil
1 tbsp Dijon mustard
3 cloves garlic, minced
Juice of 1 lemon
Juice of 1 orange
1 tsp dried basil
2 tbsp white wine (optional)

PREPARATION METHOD

Combine all ingredients together in a bowl. Add the prawns, mix well. Cover and refrigerate for 1 hour before cooking.

6 SERVES

Chicken Marinade

INGREDIENTS

1 egg
60ml Donegal Rapeseed Oil
11ml cider vinegar
½ tbsp salt
¾ tsp poultry seasoning
Pinch ground black pepper

PREPARATION METHOD

Blend all ingredients together in a food processor. Marinade the meat, cover and refrigerate for 1-3 hours before cooking.

6 SERVES

Lamb Marinade

INGREDIENTS

1 tbsp Donegal Rapeseed Oil
4 tbsp honey
2 tbsp Dijon mustard
2 tbsp rosemary
1 tsp freshly ground black pepper
1 tsp lemon zest
3 cloves garlic, minced

PREPARATION METHOD

Combine all ingredients and mix well. Apply to meat, cover and refrigerate overnight.

7 SERVES

Fish Marinade

INGREDIENTS

75ml Donegal Rapeseed Oil
75ml water
75ml vinegar
3 cloves garlic, finely chopped
1 tsp dried thyme
1 tsp dried Italian herb seasoning
1 tsp chicken seasoning
1 tsp dried rosemary, crushed
1 tsp salt
1 tsp ground black pepper

PREPARATION METHOD

Combine all ingredients in bowl and mix well. Marinade, cover and refrigerate fish for 1 hour before cooking.

4-6 SERVES

Pork Marinade

INGREDIENTS

¼ cup Donegal Rapeseed Oil
2 cups pineapple juice
3 tbsp Sriracha sauce
Salt and pepper, to taste

PREPARATION METHOD

Reduce pineapple juice by ¾ over heat and allow to cool.

Combine all ingredients together. Refrigerate half the marinade. Leave meat to marinade in remaining half, covered and refrigerated for several hours before cooking. Apply the remaining marinade to the pork at intervals while cooking.

4 SERVES

MARINADES

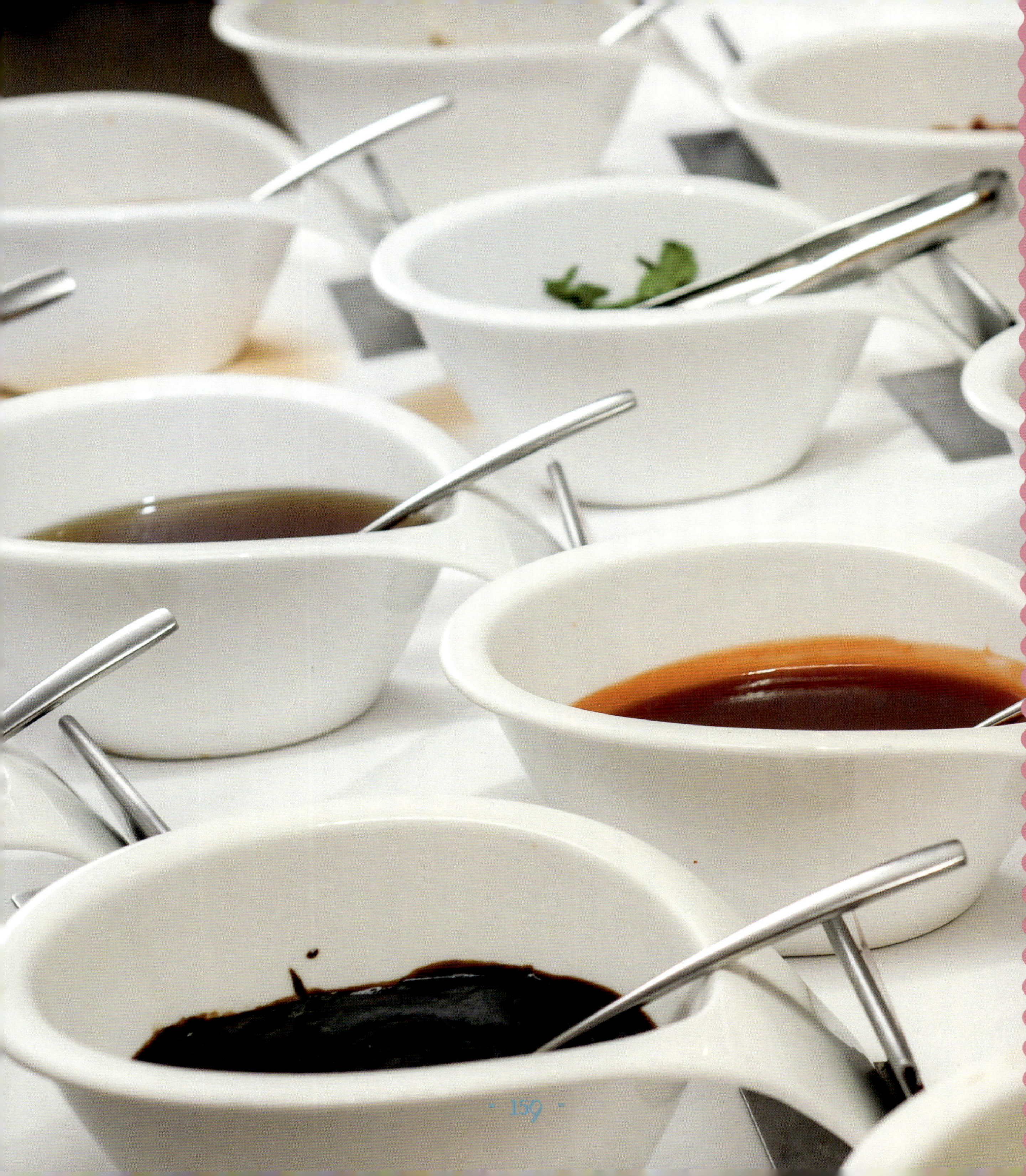

Conversion Chart

Celsius (°C)	Fahrenheit (°F)	Gas Mark
130	250	½
140	275	1
150	300	2
160	320	3
170	350	4
190	375	5
200	400	6
220	425	7
230	450	8
240	475	9
260	500	10

Metric	Imperial
1.25 ml	¼ teaspoon (tsp)
2.5 ml	½ tsp
5 ml	1 tsp
15 ml	1 tablespoon (tbsp)
60 ml	¼ cup
75 ml	⅓ cup
125 ml	½ cup
150 ml	⅔ cup
175 ml	¾ cup
250 ml	1 cup
275 ml	1⅛ cup
300 ml	1¼ cup
350 ml	1½ cup
400 ml	1⅔ cup
450 ml	1¾ cup
500 ml	2 cups

Metric	Imperial
10 g	¼ oz
15 g	½ oz
25 g	1 oz
50 g	1¾ oz
75 g	2¾ oz
100 g	3½ oz
150 g	5½ oz
175 g	6 oz
200 g	7 oz
225 g	8 oz
250 g	9 oz
275 g	9¾ oz
350 g	12 oz
450 g	1 lb

Directory

Ballymaloe Foods
Courtstown Business Park
Little Island
Co Cork
021 435 4810
www.ballymaloefoods.ie
hello@ballymaloefoods.ie

BiaMaith
www.biamaith.ie
Facebook: BiaMaith

Chef Brian McDermott
Moville
Co Donegal
074 9385921
www.chefbrianmcdermott.com
info@chefbrianmcdermott.com

The Brook Inn
Sallybrook
Glanmire
Co Cork
021 4821498
www.thebrookinn.ie
bernie@brookinn.com

The Burren Smokehouse
Lisdoonvarna
Co Clare
065 7074432
www.burrensmokehouse.com

Carl Mark O'Neill
A Day in the Life of a Food Explorer
www.irelandstableproduce.com
+353879488836

Castlemartyr Resort
Neil Ferguson
Grange
Castlemartyr
Co Cork
021 4219000
www.castlemartyrresort.ie
info@castlemartyeresort.ie

The Counter Deli
Canal Road
Letterkenny
Co Donegal
074 9120075
www.thecounterdeli.com
info@thecounterdeli.com

Drop Chef
www.dropchef.com
hello@dropchef.com

Food 4 Thought
5 Lower Abbeygate Street
The Docks
Co Galway
091 565854

I Love Cooking
13 Upper Baggot Street
Dublin 4
www.ilovecooking.ie
hi@ilovecooking.ie

Irish Food Guide
www.irishfoodguide.ie
Twitter @IrishFoodGuide

Kwanghi Chan- ChanChan Sauce
www.chanchansauce.com
Twitter @kwanghi_

The Lemon Tree Restaurant
32-34 Courtyard Shopping Centre
Lower Main Street
Letterkenny
Co Donegal
074 91 25788
www.thelemontreerestaurant.com
lemontreerestaurant@hotmail.com

Lyons Café
Quay Street
Abbeyquarter North
Co Sligo
071 9142969
www.lyonscafe.com
info@lyonscafe.com

Directory

MacNean House and Restaurant
Main Street
Blacklion
Co Cavan
071 9853022
www.nevenmaguire.com
info@macneanrestaurant.com

Mulberry Garden
Mulberry Lane
Donnybrook
Co Dublin
01 2693300
www.mulberrygarden.ie
eat@mulberrygarden.ie

Niamh McAteer
Instagram @curly_hairedfreak

Nook Café
Main Street
Collooney
Co Sligo
087 3522135
eatatnook@gmail.com
Facebook @NookCafeRestaurant

O'Connors Seafood Restaurant
Wolfe Tone Square
Bantry
Co Cork
027 55664

Rushe Fitness
Enterprise Fund Business Centre
Letterkenny
Co Donegal
086 0867953
www.rushefitness.ie
info@rushefitness.ie

Sage Restaurant
Shteryo Yurukov and Eva Ivanova
10 High Street
Westport
Co Mayo
098 56700
www.sagewestport.ie
info@sagewestport.ie

Chef Shane Smith
www.chefshanesmith.ie
Twitter: @ShaneSmith83
Facebook: chefshanesmith

Shell's Café
Seafront
Strandhill
Co Sligo
071 9122938
www.shellscafe.com
hello@shellscafe.com

The Tavern Bar & Restaurant
Myles and Ruth O'Brien
Murrisk
Westport
Co Mayo
098 64060
www.tavernmurrisk.com
info@tavernmurrisk.com

Thyme to Eat
www.thymetoeat.ie
Facebook: Thyme to Eat
Instagram: thymetoeat1
Twitter: @annakingsto
Snapchat: annajkingston

Yahi Café
Unit 11 Great Northern Mall
Belfast
Co Antrim
028 90230333
Facebook @YAHIcafe

Yeats Tavern
Drumcliff Bridge
Co Sligo
071 9163117
www.yeatstavernrestaurant.com
info@yeatstavernrestaurant.com

Recipe Index

Starters

Chicken Wings with BBQ Sauce 10 | Crab Meat, Lobster and Monk Liver Salad 18 | Creamy Wild Mushroom Tart 14 | Goats Cheese with Roasted Peppers 16 | Irish Albacore Tuna Carpaccio 20 | Marinated Heirloom Tomatoes 12 | Salmon Roulade 22 | Sizzling Garlic Chilli Prawns 26 | Thai Fishcakes 24 |

Salads

Beetroot and Goats Cheese Salad with Raspberry Dressing 28 | Chicken Caesar Salad 30 | Chicken, Couscous and Rocket Salad with Citrusy Orange 32 | Raw Beet Salad 34 | Warm Bacon and Potato Salad with Honey and Mustard Dressing 36 |

Soups

Butternut Squash, Coconut and Chili Soup 38 | Carrot and Lentil Soup 46 | Creamy Tomato Soup 44 | Minestrone Soup 40 | Roasted Sweet Potato and Carrot Soup 42 |

Mains

Bacon and Mushroom Tagliatelle 86 | Beef Fajitas 100 | Beef Lasagne 102 | Chicken Cacciatore 74 | Chicken Korma 72 | Chicken Thighs with Sweet Potatoes 62 | Chilli Beef Burger with Chilli Jam 94 | Chilli Con Carne 96 | Cod Fillets with Lemon Chive Sauce 54 | Chorizo and Salami Pizza 92 | Cream Cheese Stuffed Chicken with Mushroom Fricassee 66 | Fillet of Beef with Chunky Chips 98 | Fillet Steak with Potato Millefeuille, Crispy Onion Rings and White Truffle Butter 106 | Grilled Salmon Steaks with Hickory Smoked Butter 50 | Hearty Donegal Chicken Casserole 64 | Hong Kong Style Chicken 68 | Irish Stew 82 | Japanese Miso Ramen 76 | Lamb Curry 80 | Lobster Risotto 58 | Monkfish with Curried Mussels and Chargrilled Vegetables 56 | Pan Seared Cod, Garlic Potato and Salsa Verde 52 | Pork Belly with Apple Salad and Smoked Hickory Dressing 90 | Pork Chops with Sage Tagliatelle 88 | Ribeye Tomato Salsa and Smoky Paprika Potatoes 108 | Salmon and Leek Fishcakes 48 | Spanish Chicken Thigh and Potato Bake 60 | Thai Chicken Stir Fry 70 | The Perfect Steak 104 | Turkey Burger with Sweet Potato Fries 78 | Whole Wheat Spaghetti Carbonara 84 |

Breads, Bakes, Desserts

Apple and Donegal Rapeseed Oil Cake 132 | Banana and Walnut Bread 124 | Brown Bread 120 | Carrot Cake 128 | Cheese and Onion Yeast Bread 118 | Cheese and Seed Bread 122 | Chocolate cake 130 | Donegal Rapeseed Oil and Elderflower Jelly, Freeze Dried Strawberries, Elderflower Sorbet 112 | Donegal Rapeseed Oil, Orange and Rosemary Polenta Cake 134 | Irish Soda Bread 116 | Perfect Scones 114 | Raspberry, Coconut and lemon Loaf 126 | Strawberry Muffins 136 | White Chocolate Tart with Strawberry Lavender Compote 110 |

Recipe Index

Light Bites

Bacon 'n' Egg Muffins 142 | Baked Potato, Grated Cheddar and Ballymaloe Relish 138 | Huevos Rancheros 148 | Poached Egg on Sourdough Bruschetta 144 | Shakshuka 146 | Three Cheese Chorizo 140 |

Dressings and Dressings

Cherry Tomato Salsa 152 | Crushed Chickpeas 152 | Curry and Mango Dip 152 | Garlic Pesto 154 | Guacamole 153 | Hidden Veggie Tomato Sauce 154 | Honey and Rapeseed Oil Dressing 155 | Hummus with Garlic, Chilli and Parmesan 150 | Sundried Tomato Pesto 153 |

Marinades

Chicken Marinade 157 | Citrus and Garlic Marinade 157 | Fish Marinade 158 | Garlic and Herb Marinade 156 | Kebab Marinade 156 | Lamb Marinade 157 | Pork Marinade 158 | Steak Marinade 156 | Honey and Rapeseed Oil Dressing 155 | Hummus with Garlic, Chilli and Parmesan 150 | Sundried Tomato Pesto 153 |

Donegal Rapeseed Oil Company

DONEGAL RAPESEED OIL – AN OIL FULL OF CHARACTER WITH A STORY TO TELL…

Donegal Rapeseed Oil is locally owned and operated specialising in the manufacture of 100% pure rapeseed oil. We have used our expertise to develop an award winning range of products.

It is a home grown, cold pressed oil which reflects the character and nature of our carefully selected growers and the unique soil that they have farmed for generations. Atlantic winds and soil conditions are what make us different, with the colder climate slowing the seed maturing in the pod, giving a fuller and unique flavour to every bottle. With no additives or preservatives, our oil brings the wonderful natural taste of Donegal to your kitchen.

Donegal Rapeseed Oil is Gluten Free and Dairy Free which means it is suitable for coeliacs, vegetarians and vegans.

Our oil has a high smoke point of 240°C which means you can fry, roast or bake at a high temperature while still retaining the natural goodness of the food. It is also ideal in dressings, dips and marinades to add that warm, golden colour.

We hope that the recipes featured in this book introduce you to new ways of cooking with our products.

As they say in Donegal, **'A wee drop goes a long way!'**

Health Benefits of Donegal Rapeseed Oil

- Contains less saturated fat than all other commonly used cooking oils and fats (Less than half the saturated fat of olive oil).
- High in unsaturated fats, particularly mono-unsaturated, replacing saturated fats with unsaturated fats contributes to the maintenance of normal cholesterol levels which will reduce the risk of heart disease.
- High in Omega 3; Omega 3 is a polyunsaturated fatty acid which is an essential nutrient for good health. They are essential for normal body functioning, such as building cell membranes in the brain and also controlling blood clotting. Omega 3 cannot be made in our bodies so it is vital to get them through the foods that contain them. Including Omega 3 in your diet will protect you against heart disease and possibly strokes.
- Contains Omega 6 which is also an essential nutrient for good health. Omega 6 lowers cholesterol and reduces inflammation in the body. This Omega also protects against heart disease.
- High in Omega 9 fatty acids which are monounsaturated fats important for a healthy heart and blood sugar control. They help to reduce the risk of cardiovascular disease and stroke by increasing the good cholesterol and reducing the bad cholesterol.
- High in Vitamin E, which is a natural antioxidant, essential for healthy skin and eyesight as well as growth and reproduction.

Donegal Rapeseed Oil Company

For more information on our company, please visit our website:

www.donegalrapeseedoil.com

All Donegal Rapeseed Oil products can be ordered online at www.donegalrapeseedoil.ie or see our website for details of your local stockist.

Contact Details

Telephone: +35374 91 45386

Email: info@donegalrapeseedoil.com

@DonegalRapeseedOil

@DonegalRapeseed

@donegalrapeseedoil.

North West Labels

Make Your Message Stick

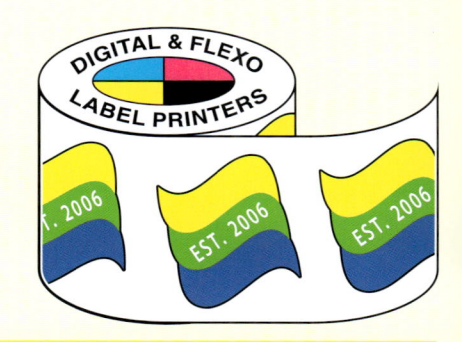

DIGITAL & FLEXO LABEL PRINTERS
EST. 2006

SERVICING THE FOOD & DRINK TRADE SINCE 2006

Find us on **f**
Facebook.com/NWLabels

Unit 10, Kilderry Business Park, Muff, Co. Donegal.
Tel: +353 (0)74 9384088
Mob: +353 (0)86 0638747
Email: sales@nwlabels.com
Web: www.nwlabels.com

H!VE
Quay Street, Donegal Town

LOCAL HONEY

100% NATURAL

WINTER COLDS & FLU'S?
H!VE ACTIVE+ HONEY

Donegal Rapeseed Oil Company
THE TASTE OF DONEGAL

www.donegalrapeseedoil.com

A GUIDE TO COOKING
with Donegal Rapeseed Oil

PERFECT FOR

- Baking
- Roasting
- Dressings
- Stir Frying
- Gluten Free
- Unique Taste

Donegal Rapeseed Oil contains no artificial colours or preservatives. Recommended by Personal Trainers and Nutritionists.

Donegal Rapeseed Oil naturally contains VITAMIN E, a powerful antioxidant that helps to protect body cells from damage.

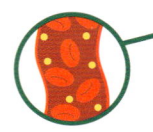

OMEGA 3 contributes to the maintenance of normal blood cholesterol levels.

SHOP ONLINE
www.donegalrapeseedoil.com